FINAL

AUTHORITY

This Is My Beloved Son In Whom I Am Well Pleased.

Hear Him!

Jesus Christ

Author

Transcribed by

A son in Christ Jesus

THE ORDER OF EVENTS

01.0	THE PLOT TO KILL JESUS	18
02.0	JUDAS AGREES TO BETRAY JESUS	20
03.0	BETRAYAL AND ARREST IN GETHSEMANE	23
04.0	JESUS FACES THE SANHEDRIN	27
04.1	Caiaphas Removed as High Priest	32
04.2	Jesus is High Priest at His Trial	35
04.3	Jesus Handed over to Pontius Pilate	46
05.0	JESUS FACES PILATE	47
06.0	JESUS TAKING THE PLACE OF BARABASS	50
07.0	THE RESURRECTION GOSPEL	53
07.1	Jesus Raises the Son of the Widow of Nain	56
07.2	Jesus Raises Jairus's Daughter	64
07.3	Jesus Raises Lazarus	71
07.4	Jesus Prayer before Raising Lazarus	80
07.5	Jesus Prays for All Believers	81
07.6	Jesus Baptizes with the Holy Spirit	82

07.7	Jesus Raises Himself from the Dead	83
07.8	Jesus Statement of Self Resurrection (The Good Shepherd)	87
07.9	Understanding the Spiritual Body (Jesus transfiguration in His Kingdom)	89
07.10	The Last Enemy That Will Be Destroyed Is Death	91
07.11	Understanding the Nature Of The Resurrection	92
07.12	The Believers Final Victory	94
08.0	THE KING ON A CROSS	95
09.0	JESUS DIES ON THE CROSS	100
10.0	JESUS BURIED IN JOSEPH'S TOMB	103
11.0	HE IS RISEN	105
11.1	Jesus is the True Shepherd	107
12.0	MARY MAGDALENE SEES THE RISEN LORD	110
13.0	JESUS APPEARS TO HIS DISCIPLES	111

14.0	THE GREAT COMMISSION	112
15.0	FINAL AUTHORITY	115
15.1	FINAL AUTHORITY RESTS	119

If you were asked to read a story about someone who had saved many peoples lives, but was now on trial for his own life. That he had said nothing but the truth but was considered to be a danger to the public and society. Most important is that what he knows could bring about a better life for you, and possibly save your life as well as the lives of others you love. Would you take the time to read his story and be willing to help if you found he was *innocent*?

Then FINAL AUTHORITY is a must read book for you. The total book is packed with facts and evidence for both sides. Yet you are the one who decides if he should be accepted or rejected by society, be believed because his actions speak louder than his words and most importantly, if he should live or die.

Here are some interesting facts about his story:

- The high court prosecutor has used his influence to bring about a consensus of guilt so politically he will remain in office.

- The legal standing of the high court prosecutor has been put in question by his actions and actually has disqualified him from continuing in his role.

- The residing Governor is concerned with how or if the people will accept him if he does not bend to the high courts will.

- The person on trial knows that his actions among the people have made him popular with them but unpopular with the political and legal establishment.

- And to make things even more tenuous for the person on trial, he is constantly being approached by the public and society leaders to demonstrate or explain where he received the knowledge or authority to save peoples lives.

- What do you think his chances of being freed are?

- This is your chance to find out and even take action that could save your life as well!

Understanding Presentation Formatting of Textual Content through;

Normal Text, other font sizes, **Bold,** *Italics* and <u>Underlining</u>

During the writing of this book, Jesus has given me several presentation ideas which will make interpretation of scriptural concepts easier to understand and follow. Let me explain through a short description.

In Short, those areas dealing with <u>**God**</u> are **Bold** and <u>**Single Bold Underlined**</u>.

Those for <u>***Jesus Christ***</u> are **Bold,** *Italics* and <u>***Double Underlined***</u>. (There may be Normal Text used, other font sizes and double underline styles, however this is the <u>*characteristic style*</u> **And** <u>**Speaking For God**</u> no Italics.)

For ***Making a Point,***   **Bold,** *Italics.*

For <u>***Stressing*** a **Point**</u>,   Normal Text, **Bold,** *Italics* and <u>*Single* **Underlined**</u>.

For Comparing <u>*Point*A</u> to meaning of <u>*Point*B</u>, Normal Text, **Bold,** *Italics* and <u>Single Underlining style</u>.

For Normal Text

An example: John 10:17 "Therefore <u>***My* Father loves *Me***</u>, because <u>***I* lay down *My life*** that ***I* may take *it again***</u>."

Jesus speaking	His **Father loves** _Him_		

"Therefore	_**My**_	**Father loves**	_Me_,
Normal	Bold	Bold	Bold
	Italics		Italics
	Double Underlining	Single Underlining	Double Underlining

Why?	_Jesus_ speaking	_lays down_	_His life_

Because	_I_	_**lay down**_	_**My life**_
Bold	Bold	Bold	Bold
Single Underlinine	Italics	Italics	Italics
	Double Underlining	Single Underlining	Double Underlining

Purpose?	_Jesus_ speaking	_may take_	_it again_. (_His life_)

---

that	_I_	_may take_	_it again_.
Bold	Bold	Bold	Bold
Italics	Italics	Italics	Italics
Single Underlining	Double Underlining	Single Underlining	Double Underlining

Try completing the thought from verse 17 above.

See how easy it is!

18 <u>No one takes it from Me, but I lay it down of Myself. I have power to lay it down, and I have power to take it again. This command I have received from My Father</u>."

The intent is to allow the reader a more fluid flow of thought from Understanding (<u>Ask</u>) to Wisdom (<u>Seek</u>) to Knowledge (<u>Knock</u>) and the connection back to Understanding is <u>through God by Prayer and Faith</u>.

These are steps Jesus used in learning from His Father and in teaching His disciples; Keep Asking, Seeking, Knocking!

Matthew 7: 7 <u>Ask, and it will be given to you; seek, and you will find; knock, and it will be opened to you</u>. 8 <u>For everyone who asks receives, and he who seeks finds, and to him who knocks it will be opened</u>.

All are applied to the following scriptures without changing the Text.

If however you like using a pencil, pen or highlighter there are plenty of scriptures still not completely charted in this book and my source book The Nelson Study Bible, New King James Version by Thomas Nelson, Inc.

Matthew 20:1 "For the <u>kingdom of heaven</u> is like a <u>*landowner*</u> who went out early in the morning to hire laborers for his vineyard. **2** Now when he had agreed with the laborers for a denarius a day, he sent them into his vineyard. **3** And he went out about the third hour and saw others standing idle in the marketplace, **4** and said to them, 'You also go into the vineyard, and whatever is right I will give you.' So they went. **5** Again he went out about the sixth and the ninth hour, and did likewise. **6** And about the eleventh hour he went out and found others standing idle, and said to them, 'Why have you been standing here idle all day?' **7** They said to him, 'Because no one hired us.' He said to them, 'You also go into the vineyard, and whatever is right you will receive.' **8** So when evening had come, the owner of the vineyard said to his steward, 'Call the laborers and give them their wages, beginning with the last to the first.' **9** And when those came who were hired about the eleventh hour, they each received a denarius. **10** But when the first came, they supposed that they would receive more; and they likewise received each a denarius. **11** And when they had received it, they complained against the landowner, **12** saying, **'These last men have worked only one hour, and you made them equal to us who have borne the burden and the heat of the day.'**

13 But he answered one of them and said, *'Friend, I am doing you no wrong. Did you not agree with me for a denarius?* **14** *Take what is yours and go your way. I wish to give to this last man the same as to you.* **15** *Is it not lawful for me to do what I wish with my own things? Or is your eye evil because I am good?'* **16** *So the last will be first, and the first last.* <u>*For many are called, but few chosen*</u>*.*"

You may be asking why this story of the laborers of the 11th hour was put at the beginning of the book. I believe Jesus Christ's' return is only a short time away and we all need to be ready and prepare. Not only for ourselves, also for those who have not heard His name or those who have forgotten Him. For His imminent return could be today! It is with this forethought I decided to ask Jesus to help me write His words in a convincing form that would appeal to everyone.

FINAL AUTHORITY was what was written across my "awakening sky" and as Christ has said to me, The water I shall give him will become in him a fountain of water springing up into everlasting life.

Amen

01.0 THE PLOT TO KILL JESUS

Matthew, Mark, Luke, John

Caiaphas was high priest from 18A.D. to 37A.D. Although both Caiaphas and Annas were called high priests, Caiaphas was officially the high priest, Annas (Caiaphas' father in law) had influence over the office of high priest. Both Caiaphas and Annas worked together with other religious leaders to take Christ by trickery, knowing they could not take Him by force without arousing the peoples' anger against them. Although Christ had full knowledge of their intent to seize Him, He also knew it was God's plan;

John 10:17 "Therefore *My* **Father loves** *Me*, **because** *I* **lay down** *My* **life that** *I* **may take** **it again**. 18 *No one takes it from Me*, **but** *I* **lay it down of Myself**. *I* **have power to lay it down**, **and** *I* **have power to take it again**. **This** **command** *I* **have received from** *My* **Father**."

John 10: 18 '*No one takes it from Me, but I lay it down of Myself.*'

Matthew

26:3 Then the *chief priests, the scribes, and the elders of the people assembled at the palace of the* **high priest***, who was called* **Caiaphas***,* 4 and *plotted* **to take Jesus by trickery** *and* **kill Him**. 5 But they said, "*Not during the feast, lest there be an uproar among the people*."

Mark

14:1 After two days it was the Passover and the Feast of Unleavened Bread. And *the chief priests and the scribes sought* how they might *take Him by trickery and put Him to death*.

Luke

22:2 And *the chief priests and the scribes sought how they might kill Him, for they feared the people*.

John

7:30 Then *they sought to take Him*: but no man laid hands on Him, because his hour was not yet come. **31** And many of the people believed on Him, and said, When **Christ** cometh, *will he do more miracles than these which this man hath done?* **32** The *Pharisees heard that the people murmured such things concerning Him*; and the *Pharisees and the chief priests sent officers to take Him*.

02.0   JUDAS AGREES TO BETRAY JESUS

Matthew, Mark, Luke

Judas had been an integral part of Christ's' disciples as the trusted treasurer. However his sin far out-weighted his integrity with money and may have been the reason for his betrayal. As one of the twelve and one of Christ's' inner circle he not only knew His movements but he hoped that by betraying Him it might move Christ to action against Israelis' enemies and establish an earthly kingdom. This can be seen in the response by those arresting Jesus in the next section and at His trial before Pilate where He answered; **John 18:36** "*My kingdom is not of this world. If My kingdom were of this world, My servants would fight, so that I should not be delivered to the Jews*; *but now My kingdom is not from here*."

God had already foretold His timing and plans through the prophetic prophecy of **Zechariah 12:12** Then I said to them, "*If it is agreeable to you, give me my wages*; and if not, refrain." So *they* weighed *out* for *my wages thirty pieces of silver*. **13** And the Lord said to me, "Throw it to *the potter*"--that princely price they set on me. So I took the *thirty pieces of silver* and *threw* them *in*to *the house of the Lord* for *the potter.*

This prophetic prophecy of Zechariahs' was made after the Babylonian captivity and between 597-538B.C. (B.C. Before Christ).

By further comparison we can see how Matthews' record of the actual betrayal by Judas, compares to that prophesied by Zechariah and their overall similarity ;

"If it is agreeable to you, give me my wages; and if not, refrain."

("*What are you willing to give me if I deliver Him to you*?");

So they weighed out for my wages

(they counted   out to him);

   thirty pieces of silver.

(thirty pieces of silver.);

   threw them   into the house of the Lord

(threw down the pieces of silver in the temple);

And

   for the potter.

(the potter's field):

Matthew 26:14 Then one of the twelve, called Judas Iscariot, went to the chief priests **15** and said, "*What are you willing to give me if I deliver Him to you*?" And they counted out to him thirty pieces of silver. **16** So from that time he sought opportunity to betray Him.

Matthew 27:3 Then Judas, His betrayer, seeing that He(Christ) had been condemned, was remorseful and brought back the *thirty pieces of silver* to the *chief priests* and *elders*, **4** saying, "<u>I have sinned</u> by <u>betraying</u> innocent *blood*." And they said, "What is that to us? You see to it!" **5** Then he ***threw*** down the pieces of silver ***in the*** ***temple*** and departed, and went and <u>hanged himself</u>. **6** But the *chief priests* took the **silver pieces** and said, "It is not lawful to put them into the treasury, because they are the price of *blood*." **7** And they consulted together and bought with them ***the potter's*** **field**, to bury strangers in. **8** Therefore that **field** has been called the **Field** of *Blood* to this day.

Romans 6: 23 For the <u>wages of sin is death</u>, ***but*** **the gift of God** is eternal **life** *in* ***Christ Jesus our Lord***.

Mark

14:10 Then Judas Iscariot, one of the twelve, went to the chief priests to betray Him to them. **11** And when they heard it, they were glad, and promised to give him money. So he sought how he might conveniently betray Him.

Luke

22:3 Then Satan entered Judas, surnamed Iscariot, who was numbered among the twelve. **4** So he went his way and conferred with the chief priests and captains, how he might betray Him to them. **5** And they were glad, and agreed to give him money. **6** So he promised and sought opportunity to betray Him to them in the absence of the multitude.

03.0   BETRAYAL AND ARREST IN GETHSEMANE

Matthew, Mark, Luke, John

Matthew

26:47 And while He was still speaking, behold, Judas, one of the twelve, with a great multitude with swords and clubs, came from the chief priests and elders of the people. **48** Now His betrayer had given them a sign, saying, "Whomever I kiss, He is the One; seize Him." **49** Immediately he went up to Jesus and said, "Greetings, Rabbi!" and kissed Him. **50** But Jesus said to him, "Friend, why have you come?" Then they came and laid hands on Jesus and took Him. **51** And suddenly, one of those who were with Jesus stretched out his hand and drew his sword, struck the servant of the high priest, and cut off his ear. **52** But Jesus said to him, "Put your sword in its place, for all who take the sword will perish by the sword. **53** Or do you think that I cannot now pray to My Father, and He will provide Me with more than twelve legions of angels? **54** How then could the Scriptures be fulfilled, that it must happen thus?" **55** In that hour Jesus said to the multitudes, "Have you come out, as against a robber, with swords and clubs to take Me? I sat daily with you, teaching in the temple, and you did not seize Me.

56 But all this was done that the Scriptures of the prophets might be fulfilled." **Then all the disciples forsook Him and fled.**

Matthew 26: **31** Then Jesus said to them, "*All of you will be made to stumble because of Me this night, for it is written: 'I will strike the Shepherd, And the sheep of the flock will be scattered*.'

Mark

14:43 And immediately, while He was still speaking, Judas, one of the twelve, with a great multitude with swords and clubs, came from the chief priests and the scribes and the elders. **44** Now His betrayer had given them a signal, saying, "Whomever I kiss, He is the One; seize Him and lead Him away safely." **45** As soon as He had come, immediately he went up to Him and said to Him, "Rabbi, Rabbi!" and kissed Him. **46** Then they laid their hands on Him and took Him. **47** And one of those who stood by drew his sword and struck the servant of the high priest, and cut off his ear. **48** Then Jesus answered and said to them, "Have you come out, as against a robber, with swords and clubs to take Me? **49** I was daily with you in the temple teaching, and you did not seize Me. But the Scriptures must be fulfilled."

50 <u>Then they all forsook Him and fled.</u>

Mark 14: 27 *Then Jesus said to them, "<u>All of you will be made to stumble because of Me this night, for it is written: 'I will strike the Shepherd, And the sheep will be scattered</u>.'*

51 Now a certain young man followed Him, having a linen cloth thrown around his naked body. And the young men laid hold of him, **52** and he left the linen cloth and fled from them naked.

Luke

22:47 And while He was still speaking, behold, a multitude; and he who was called Judas, one of the twelve, went before them and drew near to Jesus to kiss Him. **48** But Jesus said to him, "<u>*Judas, are you betraying the Son of Man with a kiss*</u>?" **49** When those around Him saw what was going to happen, they said to Him, "Lord, shall we strike with the sword?"

50 And one of them struck the servant of the high priest and cut off his right ear. **51** But Jesus answered and said, "Permit even this." And He touched his ear and healed him. **52** Then Jesus said to the chief priests, captains of the temple, and the elders who had come to Him, "Have you come out, as against a robber, with swords and clubs? **53** When I was with you daily in the temple, you did not try to seize Me. *But this is your hour, and the power of darkness*."

John

18:1 When Jesus had spoken these words, He went out with His disciples over the Brook Kidron, where there was a garden, which He and His disciples entered. **2** And Judas, who betrayed Him, also knew the place; for Jesus often met there with His disciples. **3** Then Judas, having received a detachment of troops, and officers from the chief priests and Pharisees, came there with lanterns, torches, and weapons. **4** *<u>Jesus therefore, knowing all things that would come upon Him, went forward and said to them</u>*, "<u>*Whom are you seeking*</u>?" **5** They answered Him, "Jesus of Nazareth." *Jesus said to them*, "<u>*I am He*</u>." And Judas, who betrayed Him, also stood with them. **6** Now when He said to them, "<u>*I am He*</u>," they drew back and fell to the ground. **7** *Then He asked them again*, "<u>*Whom are you seeking*</u>?" And **they said, "Jesus of Nazareth."**

8 Jesus answered, "<u>*I have told you that I am He. Therefore, if you seek Me, let these go their way*</u>," **9** <u>that the saying might be fulfilled which He spoke, "Of those whom You gave Me I have lost none</u>."

Zechariah 13: 7 "<u>Awake, O sword, against My Shepherd, Against the Man</u> who is <u>My Companion</u>," <u>Says the Lord of hosts</u>. "<u>Strike the Shepherd, And the sheep will be scattered</u>; <u>Then I will turn My hand against the little ones.</u>

10 Then **Simon Peter, having a sword, drew it and struck the high priest's servant, and cut off his right ear**. The servant's name was Malchus.

11 So Jesus said to Peter, "***Put your sword into the sheath***.

Shall I not drink the cup which My Father has given Me?"

04.0   JESUS FACES THE SANHEDRIN

Matthew, Mark, Luke, John

John 12:49 "*For I have not spoken on My own authority;* but the Father who sent Me gave Me a command, what I should say and what I should speak.   50 And *I know that* His command is everlasting life.

Therefore, whatever I speak, just as the Father has told Me, so I speak."

Matthew

26:57 And **those** who had laid hold of *Jesus* led *Him* away to **Caiaphas the high priest,** where the **scribes** and the **elders** were assembled. **58** But Peter followed Him at a distance to the high priest's courtyard. And he went in and sat with the servants to see the end. **59** Now the **chief priests,** the **elders,** and all the **council** sought false testimony against *Jesus* to put Him to **death, 60** but **found none**. Even though **many false witnesses came forward,** *they* **found none**. But at last two false witnesses came forward **61** and said, "This fellow said, 'I am able to destroy the temple of God and to build it in three days.' " **62** And **the** *high priest* arose and said to *Him,* "Do You answer nothing? What is it these men testify against *You*?" **63** But **Jesus kept silent.** And **the** *high priest* answered and said to *Him,* "I put You under oath by the living God: Tell us if You are the Christ, the Son of God!" **64** *Jesus* said to *him*, "It is as you said. Nevertheless, I say to you, hereafter you will see the Son of Man sitting at the right hand of the Power, and coming on the clouds of heaven."

65 Then (**1**ˢᵀ) the high priest tore his clothes, saying, (**2**ⁿᵈ) "He has spoken blasphemy! What further need do *we* have of witnesses? Look, now *you* have heard His blasphemy! **66** What do *you* think?" (**3**ʳᵈ) They answered and said, "*He* is deserving of death." **67** Then *they* spat in *His* face and beat *Him*; and *others* struck *Him* with the palms of their hands, **68** saying, "Prophesy to us, **Christ**! Who is the one who struck **You**?"

PLEASE NOTE!

Two very important actions have just taken place, first the high priest has torn his clothes and profaned himself; And second he has told God that He has "spoken blasphemy", remember what Jesus said;

Therefore, whatever I speak, just as the Father has told Me, so I speak.

In verse 65 you will notice the sentences and underlining, also below in parenthesis.

(Then (**1**ˢᵀ) the **high priest tore his clothes**, saying, (**2**ⁿᵈ) "He has spoken blasphemy!)

28

In the next section entitled; **04.01 CAIAPHAS REMOVED AS HIGH PRIEST OF THE SANHEDRIN**

Jesus has explained that at this point the high priests statements are no longer representative of the Priestly order as assigned by **God**. **He, the high priest,** Caiaphas, **has profaned the Levitical Law of God by tearing his clothing and accusing God of speaking blasphemy**.

Mark

14:53 And they led *Jesus* away to the *high priest*; and with *him* were assembled all the *chief priests*, the *elders*, and the *scribes*. **54** But Peter followed Him at a distance, right into the courtyard of the *high priest*. And he sat with the servants and warmed himself at the fire. **55** Now the *chief priests* and all the *council* sought testimony against *Jesus* to put Him to death, but **found none**. **56** For **many bore false witness against** *Him*, **but** *their* testimonies did not agree. **57** Then some rose up and bore false witness against Him, saying, **58** "We heard *Him* say, 'I will destroy this temple made with hands, and within three days I will build another made without hands.' " **59** But *not even then did their testimony agree*. **60** And the *high priest* stood up in the midst and asked *Jesus*, saying, "Do You answer nothing? What is it these men testify against *You*?" **61 But He kept silent and answered nothing**. Again the *high priest* asked *Him*, saying to *Him*, "Are You the Christ, the Son of the Blessed?" **62** *Jesus* said, "**I am. And you will see the** Son of Man **sitting at the right hand of the Power, and coming with the clouds of heaven**."

63 Then the *high priest tore his clothes* and said, "**What further need do we have of witnesses**? **64** *You* **have heard the blasphemy**! **What do you think**?" And they all condemned *Him* to be deserving of death. **65** Then some began to spit on *Him*, and to blindfold *Him*, and to beat *Him*, and to

29

say to *Him*, "Prophesy!" And the officers struck *Him* with the palms of their hands.

Luke

22: 66 As soon as it was day, the *elders* of the people, both *chief priests* and *scribes*, came together and led *Him* into their *council*, saying, 67 "If You are the **Christ**, tell us." But **He** said to them, "**If I tell you, you will by no means believe.** 68 And **if I also ask you, you will by no means answer Me or let Me go.** 69 **Hereafter the Son of Man will sit on the right hand of the power of God.**" 70 Then they all said, "Are You then the **Son of God**?" So **He** said to them, "**You rightly say that I am.**" 71 And *they* said, "What further testimony do *we* need? For *we* have *heard it ourselves* from **His own mouth**."

John

18:12 Then the detachment of troops and the captain and the officers of the Jews arrested *Jesus* and bound *Him*. 13 And they led *Him* away to *Annas* first, for he was the father-in-law of **Caiaphas who was *high priest* that year**. 14 *Now it was Caiaphas who advised the Jews that it was expedient that one man should die for the people*.

John

18:19 The *high priest* then asked Jesus about His disciples and His doctrine. 20 **Jesus** answered *him*, "**I spoke openly to the world. I always taught in synagogues and in the temple, where the Jews always meet, and in secret I have said nothing.** 21 **Why do you ask Me? Ask those who have heard Me what I said to them. Indeed they know what I said.**" 22 And when **He** had said these things, one of the officers who stood by struck Jesus with the palm of his hand, saying, "Do You answer the high priest like that?" **23 Jesus** answered him, "**If I have spoken evil, bear witness of the evil; but if well, why do you strike Me?**" 24 Then Annas sent Him bound to **Caiaphas** the *high priest.*

Two council members of the body who were there, but were friends and supporters of Jesus probably left after hearing the councils' immediate vote to condemn Him to death.

These two members of the **council**, Joseph and Nicodemus had not consented but had witnessed the events of the trial.

Luke

24:50 Now behold, there was a man named **Joseph**, a **council** member, a good and just man. **51 He** *had not* *consented to their decision and deed*. He was from Arimathea, a city of the Jews, who himself was also waiting for the kingdom of God.

John

7:50 Nicodemus (he who came to Jesus by night, being **one of them**) said to them, **51** "*Does our law judge a man before it hears him and knows what he is doing*?"

Note: '**one of them**' here means member of the **council**.

04.1   CAIAPHAS REMOVED AS HIGH PRIEST
Matthew, Mark, Luke, John

John 12:49 "*For I have not spoken on My own authority;* but the Father who sent Me gave Me a command, what I should say and what I should speak.   50 And *I know that* His command is everlasting life.

Therefore, whatever I speak, just as the Father has told Me, so I speak."

At this point the high priests statements no longer are representative of the Levite Priestly Order.

He, the high priest, Caiaphas by name has broken the Levitical Law of God by tearing his clothing and accusing God of speaking blasphemy.

Therefore according to ;

Leviticus 26: 46 These are the decrees, the laws and the regulations that the LORD established on Mount Sinai between himself and the Israelites through Moses.

Leviticus 21 Regulations for Conduct of Priests :

Leviticus 21: 4 Otherwise he shall not *defile himself*, being a chief man among his people, to *profane himself*.

Leviticus 21: 10 '*He who is the* high priest among his brethren, on whose head the anointing oil was poured and who is consecrated to wear the garments, shall not uncover his head nor tear his clothes;

Therefore, based on previous decisions declared by God and spoken to the high priest Aaron by Moses concerning the above stated Law, are as follows;

Leviticus 10: 6 And Moses said to Aaron, and to Eleazar and Ithamar, his sons, "Do not uncover your heads **nor tear your clothes, lest you die**, and wrath come upon all the people. But let your brethren, the whole house of Israel, bewail the burning which the Lord has kindled.

Because of the **seriousness' of the acts of the high priest**, the following example has been added of punishment for a **profane** act by two of *Aarons sons*, priests before God;

The Profane Fire of Nadab and Abihu

Leviticus 10: 1 Then Nadab and Abihu, the *sons of Aaron*, each took his censer and put fire in it, put incense on it, and offered **profane** fire before the Lord, <u>which He had not commanded them</u>. **2** <u>So fire went out from the Lord and devoured them, and they died before the Lord</u>. **3** And Moses said to Aaron, "<u>This is what the **Lord** spoke, saying:</u> **'<u>By those who come near Me I must be regarded as holy; And before all the people I must be glorified</u>**.' " So *Aaron held his peace*. **4** And Moses called Mishael and Elzaphan, the sons of Uzziel the uncle of Aaron, and said to them, "Come near, carry your brethren from before the sanctuary out of the camp."**5** So they went near and carried them by their tunics out of the camp, as Moses had said. **6** And Moses said to Aaron, and to Eleazar and Ithamar, his sons, "*<u>Do not uncover your heads</u>* **<u>nor tear your clothes, lest you die</u>**, *<u>and wrath come upon all the people</u>*. But let your brethren, the whole house of Israel, bewail the burning which the Lord has kindled. **7** You shall not go out from the door of the tabernacle of meeting, lest you die, **for the <u>anointing oil of the Lord is upon you</u>**." And they did according to the word of Moses.

04.2 JESUS IS HIGH PRIEST AT HIS TRIAL

According to the Messiah, His reign begins at this point.

To follow is His statement:

John 12: 44 Then Jesus cried out and said, "He who believes in Me, believes not in Me but in Him who sent Me. **45** And he who sees Me sees Him who sent Me.

46 I have come as a light into the world, that whoever believes in Me should not abide in darkness. **47** And if anyone hears My words and does not believe, I do not judge him; for I did not come to judge the world but to save the world. **48** He who rejects Me, and does not receive My words, has that which judges him-- the word that I have spoken will judge him in the last day. **49** For I have not spoken on My own authority; but the Father who sent Me gave Me a command, what I should say and what I should speak. **50** And I know that His command is everlasting life. Therefore, whatever I speak, just as the Father has told Me, so I speak."

Jesus is now the High Priest, prepared by _His_ Father to be Savior at the right hand of the Father in heaven and as Priest forever According to the order of Melchizedek.

Psalms 110: 1 A Psalm of David. The LORD said to my *Lord*, "Sit at My right hand, Till I make *Your* enemies *Your* footstool."

Matthew 22: 41 While the *Pharisees* were gathered together, *Jesus asked them*,

42 *saying*, "*What do you think about the* Christ? *Whose* Son *is He*?"

They said to *Him*, "*The Son* of David."

43 *He* said to *them*, "*How then does David in the* Spirit *call Him* '*Lord*,' *saying*:

44 '*The* LORD *said to my Lord*, "Sit at My right hand, Till I make *Your* enemies *Your* footstool" '?

45 "*If David then calls Him* '*Lord*,' *how is He his Son*?"

Answer :

Son of *Man* the *Lord* (*Jesus* Christ) Son of *God* the LORD
                 and **Spirit**

(**God** is LORD and **God** is **Spirit**)

(See genealogy of Jesus Christ, Matthew 1:1-16)

Psalms 110: 2 The <u>LORD</u> <u>shall send the rod of</u> *<u>Your</u>* <u>strength out of Zion</u>. <u>Rule in the midst of</u> *<u>Your enemies</u>*!

John 12:49 "*<u>For I have not spoken on My own authority</u>;* but <u>the Father who sent Me gave Me a command, what I should say and what I should speak</u>.

3 Your people shall be volunteers In the day of *<u>Your</u>* power; In the beauties of holiness, from the womb of the morning, *<u>You</u>* have the dew of *<u>Your</u>* youth. **4** The <u>LORD has sworn</u> *And* <u>will not relent</u>, "<u>You are a priest forever According to the order of Melchizedek</u>."

John 12: 50 aAnd *<u>I know that</u>* <u>His command is everlasting life</u>.

5 The <u>LORD is at</u> *<u>Your right hand</u>*; <u>He</u> shall execute kings in the day of <u>His</u> wrath. **6** <u>He</u> shall judge among the nations, <u>He</u> shall fill the places with <u>dead</u> bodies, <u>He</u> shall execute the heads of many countries. **7** He shall drink of the brook by the wayside;

Therefore <u>He</u> *<u>shall lift up the head</u>*.

John 12: 50 b*<u>Therefore, whatever I speak</u>*, <u>just as the Father has told Me, so I speak</u>."

Hebrews 7:

1 For this **_Melchizedek_**, **_king of Salem, priest of the Most High God_**,

   who met **Abraham returning from the slaughter of the kings** and **_blessed_** him,

2 **to _whom_** also **Abraham gave a tenth part of all**,

   first being translated "**_king of righteousness_**," and then also **_king of Salem_**, meaning

  "**_king of peace_**,"

3 **_without father, without mother, without genealogy, having neither beginning of_**

   days nor end of life, but made like the Son of God, remains a priest continually.

4 **_Now consider how great this man was_**, to **_whom_** even the patriarch Abraham gave a

  tenth of the spoils.

5 And **indeed those who are of the sons of Levi, who receive the priesthood, have a**

   commandment to receive tithes from the people according to the law, that is, from

   their brethren, though they have come from the loins of Abraham;

6 *but he whose genealogy is not derived from* them *received tithes from* Abraham *and blessed* him who had the promises.

7 Now beyond all contradiction the lesser *is blessed by the better*.

8 Here mortal men receive tithes, *but there he receives them, of whom it is witnessed*

   that he lives.

9 Even Levi, who receives tithes, paid tithes through Abraham, so to speak,

10 for he was still in the loins of his father when *Melchizedek* met him.

11 Therefore, if perfection were through the Levitical priesthood (for under it the people received the law), what further need was there that another *priest* should rise according to the order of *Melchizedek*, and not be called according to the order of Aaron?

12 For the *priesthood* being changed, of necessity there is also a change of the law.

13 For *He of whom* these things are spoken belongs to another tribe,

    from which no man has officiated at the altar.

14 For it is evident that our *Lord* arose from Judah,

    of which tribe Moses spoke nothing concerning priesthood.

15 And it is yet far more evident if, in the likeness of *Melchizedek*, there arises another *priest*

16 who has come, not according to the law of a fleshly commandment,

    but according to the power of an endless life.

17 For He testifies:

"*You are a priest forever According to the order of Melchizedek*."

Psalm 110: 4 The LORD has sworn *And* will not relent, "*You* are a priest forever According to the order of Melchizedek."

18 For on the one hand there is **an annulling of the former commandment** because of its weakness and unprofitableness,

Leviticus 21: 4 Otherwise he shall not defile himself, being a chief man among his people, to profane himself.

Leviticus 21: 10 '*He who is the* high priest among his brethren, on whose head the anointing oil was poured and who is consecrated to wear the garments, shall not uncover his head nor tear his clothes;

19 for the law made nothing perfect;

on the other hand, there is the bringing in of a *better hope*,

through which we draw near to God.

20 And inasmuch as *He* was not made *priest* without an *oath*

21 (for they have become priests without an **oath**,

but *He* with an *oath* by Him who said to *Him*: "The Lord has sworn And will not relent, '*You are a priest forever According to the order of Melchizedek*' "),

22 <u>by so much more Jesus has become a surety of a better covenant</u>.

23 Also <u>there were many priests, because they were prevented by death from continuing</u>.

24 <u>But *He*, because *He* continues forever, has an unchangeable priesthood</u>.

25 <u>Therefore *He* is also able to save to the uttermost those who come to God through *Him*, since *He* always lives to make intercession for them</u>.

26 <u>For such a High Priest was fitting for us, who is holy, harmless, undefiled, separate from sinners, and has become higher than the heavens</u>;

27 <u>who does not need daily, as those high priests, to offer up sacrifices, first for *His* own sins and then for the people's, for this *He* did once for all when *He* offered up *Himself*</u>.

28 <u>For the law appoints as high priests men who have weakness,</u>

<u>but the *word* of the *oath*, which came after the law, appoints the Son who has been *perfected forever*</u>.

Hebrews 9: 11 But <u>**Christ**</u> came as <u>**High Priest**</u> of the good things to come, with the ***<u>greater and more perfect</u>*** <u>tabernacle</u> not made with hands, ***that is***, <u>not of this creation</u>.

12 Not with the blood of goats and calves, *but* **with *His own blood He entered the Most Holy Place once for all, having obtained eternal redemption***. **13** For if the blood of bulls and goats and the ashes of a heifer, sprinkling the unclean, sanctifies for the purifying of the flesh,

14 *how much more shall the blood of* Christ, *who through the* eternal Spirit *offered* Himself *without spot to* God, *cleanse your conscience from* dead *fworks to serve the* living God?

15 And **for this reason** *He* is the *Mediator* of the *new covenant, by means of death, for the* **redemption of the transgressions** under the first covenant, that **those who are called may receive the promise of the** eternal inheritance.

16 **For where there is a testament, there must also of necessity be the death of the testator.** **17** **For a testament is in force after men are dead, since it has no power at all while the testator lives.**

18 **Therefore not even the first covenant was dedicated without blood.**

19 For when Moses had spoken **every precept** to all the people according to the law, he took the blood of calves and goats, with water, scarlet wool, and hyssop, and sprinkled both the book itself and all the people, **20** saying, "**This is the blood of the covenant which God has commanded you.**" **21** Then likewise he sprinkled with blood both the tabernacle and all the vessels of the ministry. **22** And **according to the law almost all things are purified with blood**, and **without shedding of blood there is no remission**.

23 Therefore <u>it was necessary that the copies of the things in the heavens should be purified with these</u>, but *<u>the heavenly things themselves with better sacrifices than these</u>*.

24 For **Christ** *<u>has not entered the holy places made with hands, which are copies of the true</u>*, but <u>into heaven itself, now to appear in the presence of</u> <u>God for us</u>;

25 *<u>not that He should offer Himself often</u>*, as the high priest enters the Most Holy Place every year with blood of another—

26 He then would have had to suffer often since the foundation of the world; but now, *<u>once at the end of the ages, He has appeared to put away sin by the sacrifice of Himself</u>*.

27 And <u>as it is appointed for men to die once</u>, <u>but after this the judgment</u>,

In the above statement, those who <u>have not</u> accepted either the Old Covenant(Mosaic Law) or New Covenant(Jesus Christ), will die and then upon Christ's return be called into judgment.

John 5: 24 "*Most assuredly, I say to you, he who hears My word and believes in <u>Him</u> who sent Me <u>has everlasting life</u>, and <u>shall not come into judgment</u>, <u>but has passed from death into life</u>.*

28 so <u>Christ was offered once to bear the sins of many</u>.

<u>To those who eagerly wait for Him He will appear a second time, apart from sin, for salvation</u>.

Hebrews 10: 19 Therefore, brethren, <u>having boldness to enter the Holiest by the blood of</u> *<u>Jesus</u>*, **20** by <u>a new and living way which He consecrated for us</u>, <u>through the</u> <u>veil</u>, <u>that is</u>, *<u>His flesh</u>*, **21** and having a <u>High Priest over the house of God</u>, **22** <u>let us draw near with a true heart in full assurance of faith, having our hearts sprinkled from an evil conscience and our bodies washed with pure water</u>.

04.3   JESUS HANDED OVER TO PONTIUS PILATE

Matthew, Mark, Luke, John

Matthew

27:1 When morning came, all the chief priests and elders of the people plotted against Jesus to put Him to death. **2** And when they had bound Him, they led Him away and delivered Him to Pontius Pilate the governor.

Mark

15:1 Immediately, in the morning, the chief priests held a consultation with the elders and scribes and the whole council; and they bound Jesus, led Him away, and delivered Him to Pilate.

Luke

23:1 Then the whole multitude of them arose and led Him to Pilate.

John

18:28 Then they led Jesus from Caiaphas to the Praetorium, and it was early morning. But they themselves did not go into the Praetorium, lest they should be defiled, but that they might eat the Passover.

05.0   JESUS FACES PILATE

Matthew, Mark, Luke, John

John 12:49 "*For I have not spoken on My own authority;* but the Father who sent Me gave Me a command, what I should say and what I should speak.   **50** And *I know that* His command is everlasting life.

Therefore, whatever I speak, just as the Father has told Me, so I speak."

Matthew

27:11 Now *Jesus* stood before the *governor*. And **the *governor*** asked *Him*, saying, "Are *You* the *King of the Jews*?" So **Jesus** said to *him*, **"It is as you say."** **12** And while *He* was being accused by the *chief priests* and *elders*, **He answered nothing**. **13** Then Pilate said to *Him*, "Do *You* not hear how many things they testify against *You*?" **14** But **He answered him not one word**, so that the governor marveled greatly.

Mark

15:2 Then *Pilate* asked *Him*, "Are *You* the *King of the Jews*?" **He** answered and said to *him*, **"It is as you say."** **3** And the *chief priests* accused *Him* of many things, but **He answered nothing**. **4** Then *Pilate* asked *Him* again, saying, "Do *You* answer nothing? See how many things they testify against *You*!" **5** But **Jesus still answered nothing**, so that Pilate marveled.

Luke

23:2 And *they began to accuse Him*, saying, "We found this fellow perverting the nation, and forbidding to pay taxes to Caesar, saying that *He Himself is Christ, a King*." **3** Then *Pilate* asked *Him*, saying, "Are *You* the *King of the Jews*?" *He* answered and said to *him*, "It is as you say."

4 So *Pilate* said to the *chief priests* and the crowd, "I find no fault in this *Man*." **5** But *they were the more fierce*, saying, "*He* stirs up the people, teaching throughout all Judea, beginning from Galilee to this place."

John

18:29 *Pilate* then went out to them and said, "What accusation do you bring against this *Man*?" **30** *They answered and said to him*, "If *He* were not an evildoer, we would not have delivered *Him* up to *you*." **31** Then *Pilate* said to them, "You take *Him* and judge *Him* according to your law." *Therefore the Jews said to him*, "It is not lawful for us to put anyone to death," **32** *that the saying of Jesus might be fulfilled which He spoke, signifying by what death He would die.* **33** Then *Pilate* entered the Praetorium again, called *Jesus*, and said to *Him*, "Are *You* the *King of the Jews*?" **34** *Jesus* answered *him*, "Are you speaking for yourself about this, or did others tell you this concerning Me?" **35** *Pilate* answered, "Am *I* a Jew? *Your* own nation and the *chief priests* have delivered *You* to me. What have *You* done?" **36** *Jesus* answered, "My kingdom is not of this world. If My kingdom were of this world, My servants would fight, so that I should not be delivered to the Jews; but now My kingdom is not from here." **37** *Pilate* therefore said to *Him*,

"Are *You* a *King* then?" Jesus answered, **"You say rightly that I am a king. For this cause I was born, and for this cause I have come into the world, that I should bear witness to the truth. Everyone who is of the truth hears My voice."** **38** Then *Pilate* said to *Him*, "What is truth?" And when *he* had said this, *he* went out again to the *Jews*, and said to them, "**I find no fault in Him at all.**

06.0   JESUS TAKING THE PLACE OF BARABASS

Matthew, Mark, Luke, John

Matthew

27:15 Now at the feast the governor was accustomed to releasing to the multitude one prisoner whom they wished. **16** And at that time they had a notorious prisoner called Barabbas. **17** Therefore, when they had gathered together, Pilate said to them, "**Whom do you want me to release to you? Barabbas, or Jesus who is called Christ?**" **18** For he knew that they had handed Him over because of envy. **19** While he was sitting on the judgment seat, his wife sent to him, saying, "<u>**Have nothing to do with that just Man, for I have suffered many things today in a dream because of Him**</u>." **20** But the <u>**chief priests and elders persuaded the multitudes that they should ask for Barabbas and destroy Jesus.**</u> **21** The governor answered and said to them, "**Which of the two do you want me to release to you?**" *They said, "Barabbas!"*

22 Pilate said to them, "**What then shall I do with Jesus who is called Christ?**" <u>***They all said to him, "Let Him be crucified!"***</u> **23** Then the governor said, "Why, what evil has He done?" <u>**But they cried out all the more, saying, "Let Him be crucified**</u>*!"*

24 When Pilate saw that he could not prevail at all, but rather that a tumult was rising, **he took water and washed his hands before the multitude, saying, "I am innocent of the blood of this just Person. You see to it."**

25 *And all the people answered and said,* "*His blood be on us and on our children.*"

26 Then he released Barabbas to them; and when he had scourged Jesus, he delivered Him to be crucified.

Mark

15:6 Now at the feast he was accustomed to releasing one prisoner to them, whomever they requested. **7** And there was one named Barabbas, who was chained with his fellow rebels; they had committed murder in the rebellion. **8** Then the multitude, crying aloud, began to ask him to do just as he had always done for them. **9** But Pilate answered them, saying, "**Do you want me to release to you the King of the Jews?**" **10** For he knew that the chief priests had handed Him over because of envy. **11** But the *chief priests stirred up the crowd, so that he should rather release Barabbas to them*. **12** Pilate answered and said to them again, "**What then do you want me to do with Him whom you call the King of the Jews?**" **13** *So they cried out again, "Crucify Him!"* **14** Then Pilate said to them, "Why, what evil has He done?" *But they cried out all the more, "Crucify Him!"* **15** So Pilate, wanting to gratify the crowd, released Barabbas to them; and he delivered Jesus, after he had scourged Him, to be crucified.

Luke

23:13 Then Pilate, when he had called together the chief priests, the rulers, and the people, **14** said to them, "**You have brought this Man to me, as one who misleads the people. And indeed, having examined Him in your presence, I have found no fault in this Man**

concerning those things of which you accuse Him; 15 no, neither did *Herod*, for I sent you back to him; and indeed nothing deserving of death has been done by Him. 16 I will therefore chastise Him and release Him" 17 (for it was necessary for him to release one to them at the feast). 18 And ***they all cried out at once, saying, "Away with this Man, and release to us Barabbas"*** 19 who had been thrown into prison for a certain rebellion made in the city, and for murder. 20 Pilate, therefore, wishing to release Jesus, again called out to them. 21 But ***they shouted, saying, "Crucify Him, crucify Him!"*** 22 Then he said to them the third time, "**Why, what evil has He done? I have found no reason for death in Him. I will therefore chastise Him and let Him go.**" 23 But ***they were insistent, demanding with loud voices that He be crucified. And the voices of these men and of the chief priests prevailed.*** 24 So Pilate gave sentence that it should be as they requested. 25 And he released to them the one they requested, who for rebellion and murder had been thrown into prison; but he delivered Jesus to their will.

John

18:39 "But you have a custom that I should release someone to you at the Passover. Do you therefore want me to release to you the King of the Jews?" **40** Then ***they all cried again, saying, "Not this Man, but Barabbas!"*** Now Barabbas was a robber.

07.0   THE RESURRECTION GOSPEL
Matthew, Mark, Luke, John

John 12:37 But although He had done so many signs before them, they did not believe in Him, **38** that the word of Isaiah the prophet might be fulfilled, which he spoke: "**Lord, who has believed our report? And to whom has the arm of the Lord been revealed?**" **39** Therefore they could not believe, because Isaiah said again: **40 "He has blinded their eyes and hardened their hearts, Lest they should see with their eyes, Lest they should understand with their hearts and turn, So that I should heal them." 41** These things Isaiah said when he saw His glory and spoke of Him. **42 Nevertheless even among the rulers many believed in Him, but because of the Pharisees they did not confess Him, lest they should be put out of the synagogue; 43** <u>for they *loved the praise of men* more than *the praise of* God</u>.

Who Has Believed Our Report?

Jesus performed so many miracles before the people of Jerusalem that He was acknowledged as a teacher sent from God. They could not deny the mighty works He performed but without the powerful grace of God in a person, even the most powerful and mighty works will not bring one to their knees or accept what they see.

To Whom Has The Arm Of The Lord Been Revealed?

As a representative of Christ and His disciples, Isaiah realized that the power of God who was the redeemer and savior of His people, by whom these miracles were performed as special operations of His grace, and would not be believed due to the blindness and hardness of their hearts. **God** determined that the only cure for them would be to "**Hear Him**!" and **believe**.

Matthew 17: 5 While he was still speaking, behold, a bright cloud overshadowed them; and suddenly a voice came out of the cloud, saying, "**This is My beloved Son, in whom I am well pleased. Hear Him**!"

Which meant a change from a self religious and arrogant people to an understanding and humble people who would **Hear *Him*** and accept the **Lord *Jesus* Christ's'** message.

Luke 6:17 And *He* came down with them and stood on a level place with a crowd of *His* disciples and a great multitude of people from all Judea and Jerusalem, and from the seacoast of Tyre and Sidon, who came to **hear *Him*** and ***be healed of their diseases***,

Luke 15:1 Then all the tax collectors and the sinners drew near to *Him* to **hear *Him***.

Luke 21:38 Then early in the morning all the people came to *Him* in the temple to **hear *Him***.

Isaiah 61: 1 "The Spirit of the Lord God is upon Me, Because the Lord has anointed Me To preach good tidings to the poor; He has sent Me to heal the brokenhearted, To proclaim liberty to the captives, And the opening of the prison to those who are bound; **2** To proclaim the acceptable year of the Lord, And the day of vengeance of our God; To comfort all who mourn, **3** To console those who mourn in Zion, To give them beauty for ashes, The oil of joy for mourning, The garment of praise for the spirit of heaviness; That they may be called trees of righteousness, The planting of the Lord, that He may be glorified."

(This is in Isaiah as the fifth of the Servant songs', this one is on the Servants mission.)

07.1   Jesus Raises the Son of the Widow of Nain

Matthew, Mark, Luke, John

Luke 7:11-17

11 Now it happened, the day after, that He went into a city called Nain; and many of His disciples went with Him, and a large crowd. **12** And when He came near the gate of the city, behold, a <u>dead</u> man was being carried out, the only son of his mother; and she was a widow. And a large crowd from the city was with her. **13** When the Lord saw her, He had compassion on her and said to her, "Do not weep." **14** Then He came and touched the open coffin, and those who carried him stood still. And He said, "*<u>Young man, I say to you, arise</u>*." **15** So he who was <u>dead</u> sat up and began to speak. And He presented him to his mother. **16** Then fear came upon all, *and <u>they glorified</u> <u>God</u>*, saying, "A **<u>great prophet</u>** *<u>has risen up among us</u>*"; *and*, "<u>God</u> <u>has visited</u> <u>His</u> <u>people</u>." **17** And this report about Him went throughout all Judea and all the surrounding region.

Understanding this Resurrection

<u>FIRST</u> we will begin by breaking out the actions Jesus took when he came upon the

Funeral scene: Luke 7:11 Now it happened, the day after, that He went into a city called Nain; and many of His disciples went with Him, and a large crowd. **12** And when He came near the gate of the city, behold, a <u>dead</u> man was being carried out, the only son of his mother; and she was a widow. And a large crowd from the city was with her.

Jesus has compassion: Luke 7:13 When the Lord saw her, He had compassion on her and said to her, "***Do not weep.***"

Isaiah 61:1 "b.To ***preach good tidings to the poor***;"

Jesus commands the dead son: 14 Then He came and touched the open coffin, and those who carried him stood still. And He said, "***Young man, I say to you, arise***."

Jesus used spoken words to raise the dead boy, what do the scriptures say concerning this action: **John 3:34 For *He* whom God *has sent speaks the* words of God, *for* God *does not give the* Spirit *by measure*. 35 *The* Father loves the Son, *and has given all things into His hand.* 36 *He who* believes *in the* Son *has* everlasting life; *and he who does not* believe *the* Son *shall not see* life, *but the wrath of* God abides on him."

Isaiah 61:1 "a.The ***Spirit of the Lord God is upon Me, Because the Lord has anointed Me***"

Jesus presents the living son to his mother: 15 So he who was dead sat up and began to speak. And He presented him to his mother.

Isaiah 61:1 "c.***He has sent Me to heal the brokenhearted***,"

SECOND, the responses of those who viewed Jesus' actions were;

The crowd: 16 Then fear came upon all, and they **glorified God**, saying, "**A great prophet has risen up among us**"; and, "**God has visited His people**."

Isaiah 61: 2 "f.*To proclaim the acceptable year of the Lord*,"

THIRD, Jesus' use of a **command** to have the young mans soul return made this resurrection the first which shows His power over death. **He is the Servant, anointed by God's Spirit to be the Anointed One and preeminent Prophet. Who speaks the words of God and is the promised Messia, Priest and King spoken of by the prophets in the Old Testament.**

It is not hard to imagine that those in a city the size of Nain, would have been quick to spread the word of this miracle and how Jesus had **command**ed the young man to **"arise"**. In fact the disciples of John the Baptist reported to him in the next two paragraphs of scripture and John responded with the following:

John 3:26 And they came to John and said to him, "Rabbi, He who was with you beyond the Jordan, to whom you have testified-- behold, He is baptizing, and all are coming to Him!" **27** John answered and said, "**A man can receive nothing unless it has been given to him from heaven. 28 You yourselves bear me witness, that I said, 'I am not the Christ,' but, 'I have been sent before Him.'**

29 He who has the bride is the bridegroom; but the friend of the bridegroom, who stands and hears him, rejoices greatly because of the bridegroom's voice. **Therefore this joy of mine is fulfilled. 30 He must increase, but I must decrease. 31 He who comes from above is above all**; he who is of the earth is earthly and speaks of the earth. **He who comes from heaven is above all. 32 And what He has seen and heard, that He testifies; and no one receives His testimony.** 33 **He who has received His testimony has certified that God is true.** 34 *For He whom God has sent speaks the words of God, for God does not give the Spirit by measure.* 35 *The Father loves the Son, and has given all things into His hand.* 36 *He who believes in the Son has everlasting life*; and he who does not believe the Son shall not see life, but the wrath of God abides on him."

Luke 7:19-23

19 And John, calling two of his disciples to him, sent them to *Jesus*, saying, "**Are *You* the Coming One, or do we look for another?**" 20 When the men had come to *Him*, they said, "John the Baptist has sent us to *You*, saying, '**Are *You* the Coming One, or do we look for another?**' " 21 And that very hour *He cured many of infirmities, afflictions, and evil spirits; and to many blind He gave sight*. 22 Jesus answered and said to them, "*Go and tell John the things you have seen and heard: that the blind see, the lame walk, the lepers are cleansed, the deaf hear, the* dead *are raised, the poor have the gospel preached to them*. 23 And *blessed is he who is not offended because of Me*."

Here Jesus has performed a miracle for this widow and her son but indicates for the first time, in His message to John that **_"blessed is he who is not offended because of Me"_**. This is Jesus' first indication that there will be those who will consider His work offensive and a sign that He, was not the anticipated political and conquering messiah the Jews are waiting for.

This miracle also demonstrates that Jesus has moved the observers to acknowledge that this boys' return to life also parallels the work of earlier prophets. However, we will notice from the details of the miracles performed by Elijah and Elisha, they **_cried out to the Lord_** and **_prayed to the Lord_**.

Elijah,

1 Kings 17:17 Now it happened after these things that the son of the woman who owned the house became sick. And his sickness was so serious that there was no breath left in him. **18** So she said to Elijah, "What have I to do with you, O man of God? Have you come to me to bring my sin to remembrance, and to kill my son?" **19** And he said to her, "Give me your son." So he took him out of her arms and carried him to the upper room where he was staying, and laid him on his own bed. **20** _Then he **cried out to the Lord** and said, "O Lord my God, have You also brought tragedy on the widow with whom I lodge, by killing her son?"_ **21** _And he stretched himself out on the child three times, and cried out to the Lord and said, "O Lord my God, I pray, let this child's soul come back to him."_ **22** _Then **the Lord heard the voice of Elijah; and the soul of the child came back to him**, and **he revived**._ **23** And Elijah took the child and brought him down from the upper room into the house, and gave him to his mother. And Elijah said, "See, your son lives!" **24** Then the woman said to Elijah, "Now by this I know that **you are a man of God**, and that **the word of the Lord in your mouth is the truth**."

And

Elisha.

2 Kings 4:8 Now it happened one day that Elisha went to Shunem, where there was a notable woman, and she persuaded him to eat some food. So it was, as often as he passed by, he would turn in there to eat some food. **9** And she said to her husband, "Look now, I know that this is a holy man of God, who passes by us regularly. **10** Please, let us make a small upper room on the wall; and let us put a bed for him there, and a table and a chair and a lampstand; so it will be, whenever he comes to us, he can turn in there." **11** And it happened one day that he came there, and he turned in to the upper room and lay down there. **12** Then he said to Gehazi his servant, "Call this Shunammite woman." When he had called her, she stood before him. **13** And he said to him, "Say now to her, 'Look, you have been concerned for us with all this care. What can I do for you? Do you want me to speak on your behalf to the king or to the commander of the army?' " She answered, "I dwell among my own people." **14** So he said, "What then is to be done for her?" And Gehazi answered, "Actually, she has no son, and her husband is old." **15** So he said, "Call her." When he had called her, she stood in the doorway. **16** Then he said, "About this time next year you shall embrace a son." And she said, "No, my lord. Man of God, do not lie to your maidservant!" **17** But the woman conceived, and bore a son when the appointed time had come, of which Elisha had told her. **18** And the child grew. Now it happened one day that he went out to his father, to the reapers. **19** And he said to his father, "My head, my head!" So he said to a servant, "Carry him to his mother." **20** When he had taken him and brought him to his mother, he sat on her knees till noon, and then died. **21** And she went up and laid him on the bed of the man of God, shut the door upon him, and went out. **22** Then she called to her husband, and said, "Please send me one of the young men and one of the donkeys, that I may run to the man of God and come back." **23** So he said, "Why are you going to him today? It is neither the New Moon nor the Sabbath." And she said, "It is well." **24** Then she saddled a donkey, and said to her servant, "Drive, and go forward; do not slacken the pace for me unless I tell you." **25** And so she departed, and went to the man of God at Mount Carmel. So it was, when the man of God saw her afar off, that he said to his servant Gehazi, "Look, the Shunammite woman!. **26** Please run now to meet her, and say to her, 'Is it well with you? Is it well with your husband? Is it well with the child?' " And she answered, "It is well." **27** Now when she came to the man of God at the hill, she caught him by the feet, but Gehazi came near to push her away. But the man of God said, "Let her alone; for her soul is in deep distress, and the Lord has hidden it from me, and has not told me." **28** So she said, "Did I ask a son of my lord? Did I not say, 'Do not deceive me'?" **29** Then he said to Gehazi, "Get yourself ready, and take my staff in your hand, and be on your way. If you meet anyone, do not greet him; and if anyone greets you, do not answer him; but lay my staff on the face of the child." **30** And the mother of the child said, "As the Lord lives, and as your soul lives, I will not leave you." So he arose and followed her. **31** Now Gehazi went on ahead of them, and laid the staff on the face of the child; but there was neither voice nor hearing. Therefore he went back to meet him, and told him, saying, "The child has not awakened." **32** When Elisha came into the house, there was the child, lying <u>**dead**</u> <u>on his bed.</u> **33** <u>He went in therefore, shut the door behind the two of them, and **prayed to the Lord**</u>. 34 *And* **he went up and lay on the child, and put his mouth on his mouth, his eyes on his eyes, and his hands on his hands;** and **he stretched himself out on the child, and the flesh of the child became warm.** **35** <u>He returned and walked back and forth in the house, and **again went up and stretched**</u>

himself out on him; then the child sneezed seven times, and the child opened his eyes. 36 And he called Gehazi and said, "Call this Shunammite woman." So he called her. And when she came in to him, he said, "Pick up your son." 37 So she went in, fell at his feet, and bowed to the ground; then she picked up her son and went out.

07.2   Jesus Raises Jairus's Daughter

Matthew, Mark, Luke, John

Matthews Account;

<u>**FIRST**</u> we will begin by breaking out the actions Jesus took when he was approached;

Matthew 9:18 While He spoke these things to them, behold, a ruler came and <u>worshiped Him</u>, saying, "**My daughter has just died, but come and lay Your hand on her and she will live.**"

We read that this was a ruler of the synagogue (Mark 5: 35), therefore a man of power and significance who approaches Jesus in a very humble manner. He prostrates himself at the feet of Jesus and expresses his strong faith and <u>worshiped Him</u>.

Jesus has compassion: Matthew 9:19 So Jesus arose and followed him, and so did His disciples.

Isaiah 61:2 "h.<u>***To comfort all who mourn***</u>,"

Matthews inner scriptural message we see a miracle occur to a woman with an issue of blood being healed by <u>touching</u> Jesus.

Matthew 9: 20 And suddenly, a woman who had a flow of blood for twelve years came from behind and **touched** the hem of His garment. **21** For she said to herself, "**If only I may touch His garment, I shall be made well.**" **22** But Jesus turned around, and when He saw her He said, "***Be of good cheer, daughter; your faith has made you well.***" And the woman was made well from that hour.

SECOND, the responses of those who viewed Jesus' actions were;

The flute players and noisy crowd: Matthew 9: 23 When Jesus came into the ruler's house, and saw the flute players and the noisy crowd wailing, **24** He said to them, "***Make room, for the girl is not dead, but sleeping.***" And they ridiculed Him. **25** But when the crowd was put outside,

THIRD, Jesus' used the touch of His hand to hers to have the young girls' soul return. This made this resurrection the second which shows ***His*** **power** over **death**.

Matthew 9: 25 *He went in and took her by the hand, and the girl arose.*

Matthew 9: 26 And the report of this went out into all that land.

Marks Account

Mark 5:21 Now when Jesus had crossed over again by boat to the other side, a great multitude gathered to Him; and He was by the sea. **22** And behold, **one of the rulers of the synagogue came, <u>Jairus</u> by name. And when he saw Him, he fell at His feet 23** and **begged Him earnestly, saying, "My little daughter lies at the point of death. Come and lay <u>Your hands on her</u>, that she may be healed, and she will live."** **24** So Jesus went with him, and a great multitude followed Him and thronged Him.

Marks inner scriptural message we see a miracle occur to a woman with an issue of blood being healed by <u>touching</u> Jesus.

Mark 5: 25 Now a certain woman had a flow of blood for twelve years, **26** and had suffered many things from many physicians. She had spent all that she had and was no better, but rather grew worse. **27** When she heard about Jesus, she came behind Him in the crowd and **touched His garment. 28** For she said, "**If only <u>I may touch His clothes</u>, I shall be <u>made well</u>."** **29 Immediately the fountain of her blood was dried up, and she felt in her body that she was healed of the affliction.** **30** And Jesus, immediately knowing in Himself that **<u>power had gone out of Him</u>**, turned around in the crowd and said, "**<u>Who touched My clothes</u>?**" **31** But His disciples said to Him, "You see the multitude thronging You, and You say, **<u>Who touched Me</u>?**' " **32** And He looked around to see her who had done this thing. **33** But the woman, fearing and trembling, knowing what had happened to her, **came and fell down before Him and told Him the whole truth. 34** And He said to her, "**<u>Daughter, your faith has made you well</u>. <u>Go in peace, and be healed of your affliction</u>.**"

Mark 5: 35 While He was still speaking, some came from the <u>ruler of the synagogue's</u> house who said, "<u>Your daughter is</u> <u>dead</u>. **Why trouble the Teacher any further?**" **36** As soon as Jesus heard the word that was spoken, He said to the ruler of the synagogue, "<u>Do not be afraid; only</u> <u>believe</u>." **37** And <u>He permitted no one to follow Him except Peter, James, and John the brother of James</u>. **38** Then He came to the house of the ruler of the synagogue, and saw a tumult and those who wept and wailed loudly. **39** When He came in, He said to them, "<u>Why make this commotion and weep</u>? <u>The child is not</u> <u>dead</u>, <u>but sleeping</u>." **40** And they ridiculed Him. But when He had put them all outside, He took the father and the mother of the child, and those who were with Him, and entered where the child was lying.

I have added a FOURTH Section to present Mark's and Luke's statements and their accounts of what occurred.

<u>FOURTH</u>, Jesus' used the **touch** of His hand to hers (v.**23**, **lay** <u>Your hands on her</u>) and the verbal **command** "<u>Talitha, cumi,</u>" which is translated, "<u>Little girl, I say to you,</u> <u>arise</u>.", to have the young girls' soul return. (the second resurrection showing <u>His</u> <u>power</u> over <u>death</u>).

41 Then <u>He took the child by the hand, and said to her</u>, "<u>Talitha, cumi,</u>" which is translated, "<u>Little girl, I say to you,</u> <u>arise</u>." **42** Immediately the girl arose and walked, for she was twelve years of age. And they were overcome with great amazement. **43** But *He commanded them strictly that no one should know it, and said that something should be given her to eat.*

67

Luke's Account;

Luke 8: 40 So it was, when Jesus returned, that the multitude welcomed Him, for they were all waiting for Him. **41** And **behold, there came a man named Jairus, and he was a ruler of the synagogue. And he fell down at Jesus' feet and begged Him to come to his house, 42 for he had an only daughter about twelve years of age, and she was dying.**

Luke's inner scriptural message we see a miracle occur to a woman with an issue of blood being healed by touching Jesus.

Luke 8: 43 Now a woman, having a flow of blood for twelve years, who had spent all her livelihood on physicians and could not be healed by any, **44** came from behind and **touched the border of His garment.** And immediately her flow of blood stopped. **45** And Jesus said, "<u>**Who touched Me**</u>?" When all denied it, Peter and those with him said, "Master, the multitudes throng and press You, and You say, '<u>Who touched Me</u>?' " **46** But Jesus said, "<u>**Somebody touched Me, for I perceived power going out from Me**</u>." **47** Now when the woman saw that she was not hidden, she came trembling; and falling down before Him, she declared to Him in the presence of all the people **the reason she had <u>touched Him</u> and how <u>she was healed immediately</u>.** **48** And He said to her, "<u>**Daughter, be of good cheer; your faith has made you well. Go in peace**</u>."

Luke 8: 49 While He was still speaking, someone came from the ruler of the synagogue's house, saying to him, "**Your daughter is dead. Do not trouble the Teacher.**" **50** *But when Jesus heard it, He answered him, saying, "<u>Do not be afraid; only</u> believe, <u>and she will be made well</u>."* **51** When He came into the house, He permitted no one to go in except Peter, James, and John, and the father and mother of the girl. **52** Now all wept and mourned for her; *but He said, "<u>Do not weep</u>; <u>she is not</u> <u>dead</u>, <u>but sleeping</u>."* **53** And they ridiculed Him, knowing that she was <u>dead</u>.

<u>FOURTH</u>, Jesus' used the <u>touch</u> of His hand to hers (v.**23, <u>lay Your hands on her</u>**) and the verbal <u>command</u> "<u>Little girl, arise</u>.", to have the young girls' soul return, (the second resurrection showing <u>His</u> <u>power</u> over <u>death</u>).

54 *But He put them all outside, <u>took her by the hand and called</u>, <u>saying</u>, "<u>Little girl, arise</u>."* **55** Then her spirit returned, and she arose immediately. And *He commanded that she be given something to eat.* **56** And her parents were astonished, but He charged them to tell no one what had happened.

Understanding the Resurrections

As we have been proceeding through these resurrections it became obvious that Jesus truly was the fulfillment of the prophecies of Isaiah's fifth song of the mission of the suffering servant. To follow below is the final fulfillment of the prophets' song **through verse 3**. This scripture was also read by Christ at His inaugural address to the beginning His ministry and is included to show how the prophets' divine oracle and Jesus ministry are linked. Lazarus resurrection is the last of the documented resurrections performed by Jesus before His own resurrection.

Isaiah 61: 1 "a.The Spirit of the Lord God is upon Me, Because the Lord has anointed Me b.To preach good tidings to the poor; c.He has sent Me to heal the brokenhearted, d.To proclaim liberty to the captives, e.And the opening of the prison to those who are bound; **2 f.To proclaim the acceptable year of the Lord,** g.And the day of vengeance of our God; h.**To comfort all who mourn, 3** i.To console those who mourn in Zion, j.To give them beauty for ashes, k.The oil of joy for mourning, l.The garment of praise for the spirit of heaviness; m.That they may be called trees of righteousness, n.The planting of the Lord, that He may be glorified."

(Above are the completed prophecies for Isaiah's Servant songs' on the Servants mission.)

07.3   Jesus Raises Lazarus
John

John 11:1 Now a certain man was sick, Lazarus of Bethany, the town of Mary and her sister Martha. **2** It was that Mary who <u>**anointed the Lord with fragrant oil**</u> and *wiped His feet with her hair*, whose brother Lazarus was sick.

Isaiah 61: 3 "k.The <u>oil of joy</u> for mourning,"

John 11:3 Therefore <u>**the sisters**</u> sent to Him, saying, "Lord, behold, he whom You love is sick." **4** When Jesus heard that, He said, "<u>***This sickness is not*** unto <u>death</u></u>,

Isaiah 61: 3 "j.To <u>give them</u> *<u>beauty</u>* for <u>ashes</u>,"

John 11: 4 *but for the <u>glory of God</u>, that the <u>Son of God may be glorified</u> through it.*"

Isaiah 61: 1 "d.<u>*To proclaim*</u> <u>liberty</u> *to the <u>captives</u>,*"

John 11: 5 Now Jesus loved Martha and her sister and Lazarus. **6** So, when He heard that he was sick, He stayed two more days in the place where He was. **7** Then after this He said to the disciples, "<u>**Let us go to Judea again**</u>." **8** The disciples said to Him, "**Rabbi, lately the Jews sought to stone You, and are You going there again?**" **9** Jesus answered, "<u>*Are there not twelve hours in the day*</u>? <u>*If anyone walks in the day*, *he does not stumble*, *because he sees the* <u>light of this world</u></u>. **10** <u>*But if one walks in the night, he stumbles, because the light is not in him*</u>."

John 11: 11 These things He said, and after that He said to them, "**Our friend Lazarus sleeps, but I go that I may wake him up.**" **12** Then His disciples said, "**Lord, if he sleeps he will get well.**" **13** However, Jesus spoke of his death, but they thought that He was speaking about taking rest in sleep. **14** Then Jesus said to them plainly, "**Lazarus is dead.**

15 And *I am glad for your sakes that I was not there, that you may believe. Nevertheless let us go to him.*"

John 11: 16 Then Thomas, who is called the Twin, said to his fellow disciples, "Let us also go, that we may die with Him." **17 So when Jesus came, He found that he had already been in the tomb four days.** **18** Now Bethany was near Jerusalem, about two miles away. **19** And many of the Jews had joined the women around Martha and Mary, to comfort them concerning their brother. **20** Then Martha, as soon as she heard that Jesus was coming, went and met Him, but Mary was sitting in the house.

John 11: 21 Then Martha said to Jesus, "**Lord, if You had been here, my brother would not have died. 22 But even now I know that whatever You ask of God, God will give You.**"

23 *Jesus said to her*, "*Your brother will rise again.*"

24 Martha said to Him, "<u>I know that he will rise again in the resurrection at the last day</u>."

25 *Jesus said to her*, "<u>I am</u> *<u>the</u>* <u>resurrection</u> *<u>and the</u>* <u>life</u>.

<u>He who</u> <u>believes</u> *<u>in Me, though he may</u>* <u>die</u>, *<u>he shall</u>* <u>live</u>.

26 *And* <u>whoever</u> <u>lives</u> *<u>and</u>* <u>believes</u> *<u>in Me shall</u>* <u>never</u> <u>die</u>.

<u>Do you</u> <u>believe</u> *<u>this</u>*?"

27 She said to Him, "<u>*Yes, Lord, I believe that You are the Christ, the Son of God, who is to come into the world*</u>."

Isaiah 61: 3 "I.The *<u>garment of praise</u>* for the <u>spirit of heaviness;</u>"

John 11: 28 And when she had said these things, she went her way and secretly called Mary her sister, saying, "The Teacher has come and is calling for you." **29** As soon as she heard that, she arose quickly and came to Him. **30** Now Jesus had not yet come into the town, but was in the place where Martha met Him. **31** Then the Jews who were with her in the house, and comforting her, when they saw that Mary rose up quickly and went out, followed her, saying, "She is going to the tomb to weep there." **32** Then, when Mary came where Jesus was, and saw Him, she fell down at His feet, saying to Him, "<u>Lord, if You had been here, my brother would not have died</u>." **33** *Therefore, when Jesus saw* <u>her weeping, and the Jews who came with her weeping,</u> <u>He</u> <u>groaned in the spirit</u> *and* <u>was troubled</u>.

Isaiah 61: 3 "i.<u>To console those who mourn in Zion,</u>"

John 11: 34 *And He said*, "*Where have you laid him?*" They said to Him,"Lord, come and see." **35** *Jesus wept.* **36** Then the Jews said, "**See how *He* loved him!**" **37** And some of them said, "**Could not this Man, who opened the eyes of the blind, also have kept this man from dying?**"

38 *Then Jesus, again* **groaning in Himself**, came to the tomb. It was a cave, and a stone lay against it.

John 11: 39 Jesus said, "*Take away the stone.*" Martha, the sister of him who was dead, said to Him, "*Lord, by this time there is a stench, for he has been* dead *four days*."

Isaiah 61: 1 "e.And *the opening* of the prison to those who are bound**;**"

40 Jesus said to her, "*Did I not say to you that if you would* believe *you would see the*   glory of God?"

41a Then they took away the stone from the place where the dead man was lying.

41b And Jesus lifted up His eyes and said, "**Father,** *I thank* You *that* You *have heard Me*. **42a** *And I know that* You *always hear Me*,

Isaiah 61: 3 "n.*The planting of the* Lord, *that* He *may be glorified*."

John 11: 42b *but because of the people who are standing by I said this, that they may believe that You sent Me.*"

Isaiah 61: 3 "m.*That they may be called trees of righteousness,*"

Romans 3: 21 But now the righteousness of God *apart from the law is revealed*, being *witnessed by the Law and the Prophets*, 22 even the righteousness of God, *through faith in Jesus Christ , to all and on all who believe.*

John 11: 43 *Now when He had said these things, He cried with a loud voice,*

"*Lazarus, come forth!*"

Isaiah 61: 1 "e.*And the opening **of the prison to those** who are bound;*"

John 11: 44 *And he who had died came out bound hand and foot with grave clothes, and his face was wrapped with a cloth.* Jesus said to them, "*Loose him, and let him Go.*"

Isaiah 61: 1 "e.*And the opening of the prison to those who are bound;*"

"*O Death, where is your sting? O Hades, where is your victory?*"

1 Corinthians 15: 55

Isaiah 61:2 "g.*And* the day of vengeance of our God;"

John 12: 30 Jesus answered and said, "*This* **voice** *did not come because of Me, but for your sake*. 31 *Now is the judgment of this world; now the ruler of this world will be cast out*.

(See Section 08.0 **THE KING ON A CROSS**, John 12:23-32)

Understanding the Resurrection Gospel

Isaiah 61: 1 "a.The Spirit of the Lord God is upon Me, Because the Lord has anointed Me b.To preach good tidings to the poor; c.He has sent Me to heal the brokenhearted, d.To proclaim liberty to the captives, e.And the opening of the prison to those who are bound; 2 f.To proclaim the acceptable year of the Lord, g.And the day of vengeance of our God; h.To comfort all who mourn, 3 i.To console those who mourn in Zion, j.To give them beauty for ashes, k.The oil of joy for mourning, l.The garment of praise for the spirit of heaviness; m.That they may be called trees of righteousness, n.The planting of the Lord, that He may be glorified."

(Above are the completed prophecies for Isaiah's Servant song on the Servants' mission.)

As we have been proceeding through these resurrections, it became obvious that Jesus truly was the fulfillment of the prophecies of Isaiah's fifth song of the Servant. Below is the beginning of the Servants mission and the scripture read by Christ at His inaugural address to His ministry. This linkage between the prophets' divine oracle and Jesus resurrection ministry was for ALL who would believe that Jesus mission of freedom from captivity meant freedom from eternal death.

Luke 4:16 So _He_ came to Nazareth, where _He_ had been brought up. And as _His_ custom was, _He_ went into the synagogue on the Sabbath day, and stood up to read. **17** And _He_ was handed the book of the prophet **Isaiah**. And when _He_ had opened the book, _He_ found the place where it was written:

18 "_The Spirit of the Lord God is upon Me,_

Because the Lord has anointed Me

To preach good tidings to the poor;

He has sent Me to heal the brokenhearted,

To proclaim liberty to the captives,

And recovery of sight to the blind,

To set at liberty those who are oppressed;

19 _To proclaim the acceptable year of the Lord._ "

20 Then _He_ closed the book, and gave it back to the attendant and sat down. And the eyes of all who were in the synagogue were fixed on _Him_. **21** And _He_ began to say to them, "_Today this Scripture is fulfilled in your hearing._" **22** So all bore witness to _Him_, and marveled at the gracious words which proceeded out of _His_ mouth. And they said, "Is this not Joseph's son?"

In the records of Isaiah and other prophets, we find a clear yet somewhat 'hidden from view' design for a **final authority** to come into existence. This final authority should pick up where God's plan of a complete solution to the problem of death had begun. God moved from the old covenant, Old Testament offering of the blood of the sin offering to the offering of His Christ, his only Son, Jesus the new covenant, New Testament offering of blood. Christ's life being accepted as atonement for the sins of His believers through a death in which He gave His life willingly for each believer.

Up to this point you have read how Jesus used a **command** to raise a person from the dead, the **commands** were either "**arise**" or "**come forth**". You may have discerned that the command "arise" was used for 'the son of the widow of Nain' and 'Jairus's daughter' both who were recently dead. Where as the **command** "**come forth**" was used for Lazarus who had been dead four days. In fact, if you recall, Jesus waited before going to resurrect Lazarus so that it was understood that Lazarus was dead by all who were present. You may also recall what Martha, the sister of Lazarus said to Jesus, "Lord, by this time there is a stench, for he has been dead four days."

What this means for us is to understand how Jesus became that **Life-Giving power** that allowed these three people to return to a normal existence. And would allow Jesus to also return from the dead and **hell** in the body he was crucified in.

The next sections go through Jesus learning these **Life-Giving** steps and the preparation for His own resurrection as outlined in His words. These are a step-by-step explanation of how Jesus attained the power of the Spirit. As he took on the role of Salvation from His Father, He also had to leave to His disciples, the understanding, wisdom and knowledge of requesting their needs through prayer. Thus believers who receive the word of God and His Grace, being united in the same faith and in the same Lord Jesus Christ receive the needed gifts of the Holy Spirit through prayer.

07.4   Jesus Prayer before Raising Lazarus

John 11: 41 Then they took away the stone from the place where the dead man was lying. **And Jesus lifted up His eyes and said,** "*Father, I thank You that You have heard Me.* **42a** *And I know that You always hear Me,* **42b** *but because of the people who are standing by I said this, that they may believe that You sent Me.*"

07.5   Jesus Prays for All Believers

John 17: 20 "I do not pray for these alone, but also for those who will believe in Me through their word; **21** that they all may be one, as You, Father, are in Me, and I in You; that they also may be one in Us, that the world may believe that You sent Me.

22 And the glory which You gave Me I have given them, that they may be one just as We are one: **23** I in them, and You in Me; that they may be made perfect in one, and that the world may know that You have sent Me, and have loved them as You have loved Me. **24** Father, I desire that they also whom You gave Me may be with Me where I am, that they may behold My glory which You have given Me; for You loved Me before the foundation of the world. **25** O righteous Father! The world has not known You, but I have known You; and these have known that You sent Me. **26** And I have declared to them Your name, and will declare it, that the love with which You loved Me may be in them, and I in them."

07.6 Jesus Baptizes with the Holy Spirit

John 1: 29 The next day John saw *Jesus* coming toward him, and said, "<u>Behold</u>! <u>The Lamb of God who takes away the sin of the world</u>! 30 This is *He* of whom I said, 'After me comes a *Man* who is preferred before me, for *He* was before me.' 31 I did not know *Him*; but that *He* should be revealed to Israel, <u>therefore I came baptizing with water</u>." 32 And John bore witness, saying, "<u>I saw the Spirit descending from heaven like a dove, and He remained upon Him</u>. 33 I did not know *Him*, but *He* who sent me to baptize with water said to me, '<u>Upon whom you see the Spirit descending, and remaining on Him, this is He who baptizes with the Holy Spirit</u>.' 34 And *<u>I have seen and testified that this is the Son of God</u>*."

Galations 3: 26 For you are all sons of God through faith in Christ Jesus.

Galations 4: 6 *And* because you are sons, God has sent forth the Spirit of His Son into your hearts, crying out, "Abba, Father!"

Romans 8: 14 For as many as are led by the Spirit of God, these are sons of God.

07.7 Jesus Raises Himself from the Dead

Matthew, Mark, Luke, John

The Preparation

John 5: 1 After this there was a feast of the Jews, and Jesus went up to Jerusalem.

2 Now there is in Jerusalem by the Sheep Gate a pool, which is called in Hebrew, Bethesda, having five porches. **3** In these lay a great multitude of sick people, blind, lame, paralyzed, waiting for the moving of the water. **4** For an angel went down at a certain time into the pool and stirred up the water; then whoever stepped in first, after the stirring of the water, was made well of whatever disease he had. **5** Now a certain man was there who had an infirmity thirty-eight years. **6** When Jesus saw him lying there, and knew that he already had been in that condition a long time, He said to him, "***Do you want to be made well?***" **7** The sick man answered Him, "Sir, I have no man to put me into the pool when the water is stirred up; but while I am coming, another steps down before me." **8** Jesus said to him, "***Rise, take up your bed and walk.***" **9** And immediately the man was made well, took up his bed, and walked. And that day was the Sabbath. **10** The Jews therefore said to him who was cured, "It is the Sabbath; it is not lawful for you to carry your bed." **11** He answered them, "He who made me well said to me, 'Take up your bed and walk.'" **12** Then they asked him, "Who is the Man who said to you, 'Take up your bed and walk'?" **13** But the one who was healed did not know who it was, for Jesus had withdrawn, a multitude being in that place. **14** Afterward Jesus found him in the temple, and said to him, "***See, you have been made well. Sin no***

more, lest a worse thing come upon you." **15** The man departed and told the Jews that it was Jesus who had made him well. **16** *For this reason the Jews persecuted Jesus, and sought to kill Him, because He had done these things on the Sabbath.*

17 *But Jesus answered them,* "*My Father has been working until now, and I have been working.*" **18** Therefore the Jews sought *all the more to kill Him, because He not only broke the Sabbath, but also said that God was His Father, making Himself equal with God.*

19 *Then Jesus answered and said to them, "Most assuredly, I say to you, the Son can do nothing of Himself, but what He sees the Father do; for whatever He does, the Son also does in like manner.*

20 *For the Father loves the Son, and shows Him all things that He Himself does; and He will show Him greater works than these, that you may marvel.*

21 *For as the Father raises the dead and gives life to them, even so the Son gives life to whom He will.*

22 *For the Father judges no one, but has committed all judgment to the Son,*

23 *that all should honor the Son just as they honor the Father.*

He who does not honor the Son does not honor the Father who sent Him.

24 "*Most assuredly, I say to you, he who hears My word and believes in Him who sent Me has everlasting life, and shall not come into judgment, but has passed from death into life.*

25 *Most assuredly, I say to you, the hour is coming, and now is, when the* dead *will hear the voice of the* Son of God; *and those who hear will* live.

26 *For as the* Father *has* life in Himself, *so* He *has granted the* Son *to have* life in Himself,

27 *and has given Him* authority to execute judgment *also, because* He is the Son of Man.

28 *Do not marvel at this; for the hour is coming in which all who are in the* graves *will hear His voice*

29 *and* come forth—those who have done good, to the resurrection of life, *and* those who have done evil, to the resurrection of condemnation.

30 *I can of Myself do nothing. As I hear, I judge; and My judgment is righteous, because I do not seek My own will but the will of the* Father *who sent Me*.

31 "*If I bear witness of Myself, My witness is not true*. 32 *There is another who bears witness of Me, and I know that the witness which* He *witnesses of Me is true*.

33 You have sent to John, and he has borne witness to the truth. **34** Yet I do not receive testimony from man, but I say these things that you may be saved. **35** He was the burning and shining lamp, and you were willing for a time to rejoice in his light.

36 But *I have a greater witness than John's; for the works which the* **Father** *has given Me to finish--the very works that I do--bear witness of Me, that the* **Father** *has sent Me*. **37** And *the* **Father Himself***, who sent Me, has testified of Me.*

You have neither heard **His voice** *at any time, nor seen* **His form**. **38** *But you do not have* **His word** *abiding in you, because whom* **He sent, Him you do not believe**. **39** *You search the Scriptures, for in them you think you have* **eternal life***; and these are they which testify of Me*.

40 *But you are not willing to come to Me that you may have* **life**.

41 *I do not receive honor from men*. **42** *But I know you, that you do not have the* **love of God** *in you*. **43** *I have come in My* **Father's** *name, and you do not receive Me; if another comes in his own name, him you will receive*. **44** *How can you believe, who receive honor from one another, and do not seek the honor that comes from the only* **God**?

45 *Do not think that I shall accuse you to the* **Father***; there is one who accuses you--Moses, in whom you trust*. **46** *For if you believed Moses, you would believe Me; for he wrote about Me*. **47** *But if you do not believe his writings, how will you believe* **My words**?"

07.8   Jesus Statement of Self Resurrection

(The Good Shepherd)

John 10: 7 _Then Jesus said to them again_, "Most assuredly, _I say to you_, _I am the door_ _of the sheep_. 8 _All who ever came before Me are thieves and robbers, but the sheep did not hear them_. 9 _I am the door_. _If anyone_ _enters by Me_, _he will be saved_, and _will go in and out and find pasture_.

John 10:10 The thief does not come except to _steal_, and to _kill_, and to _destroy_. _I have come that they may have life, and that they may have it more abundantly_. 11 _I am the good shepherd_. _The good shepherd gives His life for the sheep_. 12 But a hireling, he who is not the shepherd, one who does not own the sheep, sees the wolf coming and leaves the sheep and flees; and the wolf catches the sheep and scatters them. 13 The hireling flees because he is a hireling and does not care about the sheep. 14 _I am the good shepherd_; and _I know My sheep_, and _am known by My own_. 15 As the Father _knows Me, even so_ I _know the_ Father; and _I lay down My life for the sheep_. 16 And _other sheep_ I _have which are not of this fold; them also_ I _must bring, and they will hear My voice; and there will be one flock and one shepherd_.

17 *Therefore My Father loves Me, because I lay down My life that I may take it again.*

John 5: 20 *For the Father loves the Son, and shows Him all things that He Himself does; and He will show Him greater works than these, that you may marvel.* 21 *For as the Father raises the dead and gives life to them, even so the Son gives life to whom He will.*

18 a*No one takes it from Me, but I lay it down of Myself. I have power to lay it down, and I have power to take it again.*

John 5: 24 "*Most assuredly, I say to you, he who hears My word and believes in Him who sent Me has everlasting life, and shall not come into judgment, but has passed from death into life.* 25 *Most assuredly, I say to you, the hour is coming, and now is, when the dead will hear the voice of the Son of God; and those who hear will live.*

18 b*This command I have received from My Father.*"

John 5: 26 *For as the Father has life in Himself, so He has granted the Son to have life in Himself,* 27 *and has given Him authority to execute judgment also, because He is the Son of Man.* 28 *Do not marvel at this; for the hour is coming in which all who are in the graves will hear His voice* 29 *and come forth*—those who have done good, to the resurrection of life, *and those who have done evil, to the resurrection of condemnation.*

John 11: 25 Jesus said to her, "*I am the resurrection and the life. He who believes in Me, though he may die, he shall live.* 26 *And whoever lives and believes in Me shall never die. Do you believe this?*"

07.9 Understanding the Spiritual Body

(Jesus transfiguration in His Kingdom)

In this transfiguration the three apostles Peter, James and John saw a preview of the Kingdom. The Old Testament prophets Moses and Elijah represented those of the Old Testament scriptures who were looking to the future event of the Messiah and His Kingdom.

Matthew 16: 28 *Assuredly, I say to you, there are some standing here who shall not taste* death *till they see the Son of Man coming in His kingdom."*

Matthew 17: 1 Now after six days Jesus took Peter, James, and John his brother, led them up on a high mountain by themselves;

2 *and He was* transfigured *before them*. *His* face shone like the sun, *and His* clothes became as white as the light.

3 *And behold*, Moses and Elijah appeared to them, talking with *Him*.

4 Then Peter answered and said to Jesus, "**Lord, it is good for us to be here; if You wish, let us make here three tabernacles: one for You, one for Moses, and one for Elijah.**" **5** While he was still speaking, behold, a **bright cloud** overshadowed them; and suddenly a **voice** came out of the **cloud, saying,** "**This is My beloved Son, in whom I am well pleased. Hear Him**!" **6** And when the disciples heard it, they fell on their faces and were greatly afraid. **7** But Jesus came and touched them and said, "*Arise, and do not be afraid*."

8 When they had lifted up their eyes, they saw no one but Jesus only. **9** Now as they came down from the mountain, Jesus commanded them, saying, "*Tell the vision to no one until the Son of Man is risen from the* dead."

10 And His disciples asked Him, saying, "**Why then do the scribes say that Elijah must come first?**" **11** Jesus answered and said to them, "*Indeed, Elijah is coming first and will restore all things*. **12** *But I say to you that Elijah has come already, and they did not know him but did to him whatever they wished. Likewise the Son of Man is also about to suffer at their hands*."

13 Then the disciples understood that He spoke to them of John the Baptist.

07.10   The Last Enemy That Will Be Destroyed Is Death

1 Corinthians 15: 20 *But now* Christ *is risen from the* dead, *and has become the* firstfruits *of those who have fallen asleep*. 21 *For since by man came* death, *by Man also came the* resurrection *of the* dead. 22 *For as in* Adam *all* die, *even so in* Christ *all shall be made alive*. 23 *But each one in his own order*: Christ *the* firstfruits, afterward *those who are* Christ's *at* His *coming*. 24 *Then* comes the end, *when* He delivers the kingdom to God the Father, *when* He puts an end to all rule *and* all authority *and* power.

25 *For* He must reign till He has put all enemies under *His* feet. 26 The last enemy that will be destroyed is *death*. 27 *For "*He has put all things under *His feet*." *But when* He *says "all things are put under Him*," *it is evident that* He who put all things *under Him* is excepted. 28 *Now when all things are made* subject to Him, *then the* Son Himself will also be subject *to* Him *who put* all things under Him, that God may be all in all.

07.11   Understanding the Nature Of The Resurrection

When Jesus said the following words, they were just before His arrest and crucifixion. These words give us His principle of nature that is also true for us spiritually. He is the grain of wheat and that if He does not die He abides alone. But if He dies He will produce much grain, which are lives turned to the salvation of God, for eternal life in Christ Jesus.

John 12: 23 But Jesus answered them, saying, "**The hour has come that the <u>Son of Man</u> should be glorified.** **24** **Most assuredly, I say to you, <u>unless a grain of wheat falls into the ground and</u> <u>dies</u>, <u>it remains alone</u>; <u>but if it</u> <u>dies</u>, <u>it produces much grain</u>. 25 <u>He who loves his life will lose it</u>, and <u>he who hates his life in this world will keep it for</u> <u>eternal life</u>. 26 <u>If anyone serves Me, let him follow Me; and where I am, there My servant will be also. If anyone serves Me, him My</u> <u>Father</u> <u>will honor.</u>**

1 Corinthians 15: 38 But God gives it a body as He pleases, and to each seed its own body. **39** All flesh is not the same flesh, but there is one kind of flesh of men, another flesh of animals, another of fish, and another of birds. **40** There are also celestial bodies and terrestrial bodies; but the glory of the celestial is one, and the glory of the terrestrial is another. **41** There is one glory of the sun, another glory of the moon, and another glory of the stars; for one star differs from another star in glory.

42 So also is the resurrection of the dead. *The body is sown in corruption, it is raised in incorruption.* **43** *It is sown in dishonor, it is raised in glory. It is sown in weakness, it is raised in power.* **44** *It is sown a natural body, it is raised a spiritual body. There is a natural body*, and *there is a spiritual body*.

1 Corinthians 15: **45** And so it is written, "The *first man* Adam became *a living being*." The *last Adam* became a life-giving spirit. **46** However, the spiritual is not first, but the natural, and afterward the spiritual.

47 The *first man* was of the earth, made of dust; the *second Man* is the Lord from heaven.

48 *As was the man of dust, so also are those who are made of dust*; and *as is the heavenly Man, so also are those who are heavenly*.

49 And *as we have borne the image of the man of dust, we shall also bear the image of the* heavenly Man.

07.12   The Believers Final Victory

1 Corinthians 15: 50 *Now this I say, brethren, that flesh and blood cannot inherit the kingdom of God; nor does corruption inherit incorruption.*

1 Corinthians 15: 51 *Behold, I tell you a mystery*: *We shall not all sleep, but we shall all be changed* 52 *in a moment, in the twinkling of an eye, at the last trumpet. For the trumpet will sound*, *and the dead will be raised incorruptible, and we shall be changed.* 53 For this corruptible must put on incorruption, and this mortal must put on immortality. 54 So when this corruptible has put on incorruption, and this mortal has put on immortality, then shall be brought to pass the saying that is written:

"**Death is swallowed up in Victory.**"

1 Corinthians 15: 55 "*O Death, where is your sting*? *O Hades, where is your victory*?"

56 The *sting of death is* sin, and the *strength of* sin *is the* law.

57 *But* **thanks be to God, who gives us the Victory through our Lord Jesus Christ.**

58 Therefore, my beloved brethren, **be steadfast, immovable, always abounding in the work of the Lord, knowing that your labor is not in vain in the Lord**.

Romans 8: 11 *But if the* Spirit of Him *who raised Jesus from the dead dwells in you*, He who raised Christ from the dead will also give life to your mortal bodies through His Spirit who dwells in you.

08.0 THE KING ON A CROSS
Matthew, Mark, Luke, John

<u>For if they do these things in the green wood, what will be done in the dry</u>?

John 12:23 But Jesus answered them, saying, "The hour has come that the Son of Man should be glorified. **24** Most assuredly, I say to you, unless a grain of wheat falls into the ground and dies, it remains alone; but if it dies, it produces much grain. **25** He who loves his life will lose it, and he who hates his life in this world will keep it for eternal life. **26** If anyone serves Me, let him follow Me; and where I am, there My servant will be also. If anyone serves Me, him My Father will honor. **27** "Now My soul is troubled, and what shall I say? 'Father, save Me from this hour'? But for this purpose I came to this hour. **28** Father, glorify Your name." Then a voice came from heaven, saying, "<u>I have both glorified it and will glorify it again</u>." **29** Therefore the people who stood by and heard it said that it had thundered. Others said, "An angel has spoken to Him." **30** Jesus answered and said, "<u>*This* **voice** *did not come because of Me, but for your sake*</u>. **31** <u>*Now is the judgment of this world; now the ruler of this world will be cast out*</u>. **32** <u>*And I , if I am lifted up from the earth, will draw all peoples to Myself*</u>."

Matthew

27:32 Now as they came out, they found a man of Cyrene, Simon by name. Him they compelled to bear His cross. **33** And when they had come to a place called Golgotha, that is to say, Place of a Skull, **34** they gave Him sour wine mingled with gall to drink. But when He had tasted it, He would not drink. **35** Then they crucified Him, and divided His garments, casting lots, that it might be fulfilled which was spoken by the prophet: "They divided My garments among them, And for My clothing they cast lots." **36** Sitting down, they kept watch over Him there. **37** And they put up over His head the accusation written against Him: THIS IS JESUS THE KING OF THE JEWS. **38** Then two robbers were crucified with Him, one on the right and another on the left. **39** And those who passed by blasphemed Him, wagging their heads **40** and saying, "You who destroy the temple and build it in three days, save Yourself! If You are the Son of God, come down from the cross." **41** Likewise the chief priests also, mocking with the scribes and elders, said, **42** "He saved others; Himself He cannot save. If He is the King of Israel, let Him now come down from the cross, and we will believe Him. **43** He trusted in God; let Him deliver Him now if He will have Him; for He said, 'I am the Son of God.' " **44** Even the robbers who were crucified with Him reviled Him with the same thing

Mark

15:21 Then they compelled a certain man, Simon a Cyrenian, the father of Alexander and Rufus, as he was coming out of the country and passing by, to bear His cross. **22** And they brought Him to the place Golgotha, which is translated, Place of a Skull. **23** Then they gave Him wine mingled with myrrh to drink, but He did not take it.

24 And when they crucified Him, they divided His garments, casting lots for them to determine what every man should take. **25** Now it was the third hour, and they crucified Him. **26** And the inscription of His accusation was written above: THE KING OF THE JEWS. **27** With Him they also crucified two robbers, one on His right and the other on His left. **28** So the Scripture was fulfilled which says, "And He was numbered with the transgressors." **29** And those who passed by blasphemed Him, wagging their heads and saying, "Aha! You who destroy the temple and build it in three days, **30** save Yourself, and come down from the cross!" **31** Likewise the chief priests also, mocking among themselves with the scribes, said, "He saved others; Himself He cannot save. **32** Let the Christ, the King of Israel, descend now from the cross, that we may see and believe." Even those who were crucified with Him reviled Him.

Luke

23:26 Now as they led Him away, they laid hold of a certain man, Simon a Cyrenian, who was coming from the country, and on him they laid the cross that he might bear it after Jesus. **27** And a great multitude of the people followed Him, and women who also mourned and lamented Him. **28** But *Jesus, turning to them, said, "Daughters of Jerusalem, do not weep for Me, but weep for yourselves and for your children.* **29** *For indeed the days are coming in which they will say, 'Blessed are the barren, wombs that never bore, and breasts which never nursed!'* **30** *Then they will begin 'to say to the mountains, "Fall on us!" and to the hills, "Cover us!"'* **31** *For if they do these things in the green wood, what will be done in the dry*?" **32** There were also two others, criminals, led with Him to be put to death. **33** And when they had come to the place called Calvary, there they crucified Him, and the criminals, one on the right hand and the other on the left. **34** Then <u>**Jesus said,**</u> <u>**"Father, forgive them, for they do not know what they do**</u>**."** And they divided His garments and cast lots. **35** And the people stood looking on. But even the rulers with them sneered, saying, "He saved others; let Him save Himself if He is the Christ, the chosen of God." **36** The soldiers also mocked Him, coming and offering Him sour wine, **37** and saying, "If You are the King of the Jews, save Yourself." **38** And an inscription also was written over Him in letters of Greek, Latin, and Hebrew: **THIS IS THE KING OF THE JEWS**.

39 Then one of the criminals who were hanged blasphemed Him, saying, "If You are the Christ, save Yourself and us." **40** But the other, answering, rebuked him, saying, **"Do you not even fear God, seeing you are under the same condemnation?** **41** And **we indeed justly, for we receive the due reward of our deeds; but this Man has done nothing wrong."** **42** Then he said to Jesus, **"Lord, remember me when You come into Your kingdom."** **43** And <u>**Jesus**</u> <u>**said to him**</u>**,** <u>**"Assuredly, I say to you, today you will be with Me in**</u> <u>**Paradise**</u>**."**

John

19:17 And He, bearing His cross, went out to a place called the Place of a Skull, which is called in Hebrew, Golgotha, **18** where they crucified Him, and two others with Him, one on either side, and Jesus in the center. **19** Now Pilate wrote a title and put it on the cross. And the writing was: JESUS OF NAZARETH, THE KING OF THE JEWS. **20** Then many of the Jews read this title, for the place where Jesus was crucified was near the city; and it was written in Hebrew, Greek, and Latin. **21** <u>Therefore the **chief priests** of the Jews said to</u> <u>Pilate</u>**,** <u>**"Do not write, 'The King of the Jews,' but, 'He said, "I am the**</u>

King of the Jews." ' " **22** *Pilate answered, "What I have written, I have written."* **23** Then the soldiers, when they had crucified Jesus, took His garments and made four parts, to each soldier a part, and also the tunic. Now the tunic was without seam, woven from the top in one piece. **24** They said therefore among themselves, "Let us not tear it, but cast lots for it, whose it shall be," that the Scripture might be fulfilled which says: "They divided My garments among them, And for My clothing they cast lots." Therefore the soldiers did these things. **25** Now there stood by the cross of Jesus His mother, and His mother's sister, Mary the wife of Clopas, and Mary Magdalene. **26** When *Jesus therefore saw His mother, and the disciple whom He loved standing by, He said to His mother,* "*Woman, behold your son*!" **27** Then *He said to the disciple,* "*Behold your mother*!" And *from that hour that disciple took her to his own home.*

09.0 JESUS DIES ON THE CROSS
Matthew, Mark, Luke, John

Matthew

27:45 Now from the sixth hour until the ninth hour there was darkness over all the land. **46** And <u>*about the ninth hour* Jesus *cried out with a loud voice, saying,* "*Eli, Eli, lama sabachthani?*" *that is,* "*My God, My God, why have You forsaken Me*</u>?" **47** Some of those who stood there, when they heard that, said, "This Man is calling for Elijah!" **48** Immediately one of them ran and took a sponge, filled it with sour wine and put it on a reed, and offered it to Him to drink. **49** The rest said, "Let Him alone; let us see if Elijah will come to save Him." **50** And <u>*Jesus cried out again with a loud voice, and yielded up His spirit*</u>. **51** <u>*Then, behold, the veil of the temple was torn in two from top to bottom; and the earth quaked, and the rocks were split*</u>, **52** and <u>*the graves were opened; and many bodies of the saints who had fallen asleep were raised*</u>; **53** and <u>**coming out of the graves after His resurrection**, **they went into the holy city and appeared to many**</u>. **54** So when the centurion and those with him, who were guarding Jesus, saw the earthquake and the things that had happened, they feared greatly, saying, "**Truly this was the Son of God!**" **55** And many women who followed Jesus from Galilee, ministering to Him, were there looking on from afar,

Mark

15:33 Now when the sixth hour had come, there was darkness over the whole land until the ninth hour. **34** And <u>*at the ninth hour* Jesus *cried out with a loud voice, saying,* "*Eloi, Eloi, lama sabachthani?*" *which is translated,* "*My God, My God, why have You forsaken*</u>

Me?" **35** Some of those who stood by, when they heard that, said, "Look, He is calling for Elijah!" **36** Then someone ran and filled a sponge full of sour wine, put it on a reed, and offered it to Him to drink, saying, "Let Him alone; let us see if Elijah will come to take Him down." **37** And *<u>Jesus cried out with a loud voice, and breathed His last</u>*. **38** Then the veil of the temple was torn in two from top to bottom. **39** So when the centurion, who stood opposite Him, saw that He cried out like this and breathed His last, he said, "**Truly this Man was the Son of God!**" **40** There were also women looking on from afar, among whom were Mary Magdalene, Mary the mother of James the Less and of Joses, and Salome, **41** who also followed Him and ministered to Him when He was in Galilee, and many other women who came up with Him to Jerusalem.

Luke

23:44 Now it was about the sixth hour, and there was darkness over all the earth until the ninth hour. **45** Then the sun was darkened, and the veil of the temple was torn in two. **46** And *<u>when Jesus had cried out with a loud voice, He said</u>*, "*<u>Father, 'into Your hands I commit My spirit.'</u>* " *<u>Having said this, He breathed His last</u>*. **47** So when the centurion saw what had happened, he glorified God, saying, "**Certainly this was a righteous Man!**" **48** And the whole crowd who came together to that sight, seeing what had been done, beat their breasts and returned. **49** But all His acquaintances, and the women who followed Him from Galilee, stood at a distance, watching these things.

John

19:28 After this, Jesus, knowing that all things were now accomplished, that the Scripture might be fulfilled, said, "*I thirst*!" **29** Now a vessel full of sour wine was sitting there; and they filled a sponge with sour wine, put it on hyssop, and put it to His mouth. **30** So when Jesus had received the sour wine, *He said*, "*It is finished*!" *And bowing His head, He gave up His spirit*.

10.0 JESUS BURIED IN JOSEPH'S TOMB
Matthew, Mark, Luke, John

Matthew

27:57 Now when evening had come, there came a rich man from Arimathea, named Joseph, who himself had also become a disciple of Jesus. **58** This man went to Pilate and asked for the body of Jesus. Then Pilate commanded the body to be given to him. **59** When Joseph had taken the body, he wrapped it in a clean linen cloth, **60** and laid it in his new tomb which he had hewn out of the rock; and he rolled a large stone against the door of the tomb, and departed. **61** And Mary Magdalene was there, and the other Mary, sitting opposite the tomb.

Mark

15:42 Now when evening had come, because it was the Preparation Day, that is, the day before the Sabbath, **43** Joseph of Arimathea, a prominent council member, who was himself waiting for the kingdom of God, coming and taking courage, went in to Pilate and asked for the body of Jesus. **44** *Pilate marveled that He was already dead; and summoning the centurion, he asked him if He had been dead for some time. 45 So when he found out from the centurion, he granted the body to Joseph*. **46** Then he bought fine linen, took Him down, and wrapped Him in the linen. And he laid Him in a tomb which had been hewn out of the rock, and rolled a stone against the door of the tomb. **47** And Mary Magdalene and Mary the mother of Joses observed where He was laid.

Luke

23:50 Now behold, there was a man named Joseph, a council member, a good and just man. **51** He had not consented to their decision and deed. He was from Arimathea, a city of the Jews, who himself was also waiting for the kingdom of God. **52** This man went to Pilate and asked for the body of Jesus. **53** Then he took it down, wrapped it in linen, and laid it in a tomb that was hewn out of the rock, where no one had ever lain before. **54** That day was the Preparation, and the Sabbath drew near. **55** And the women who had come with Him from Galilee followed after, and they observed the tomb and how His body was laid. **56** Then they returned and prepared spices and fragrant oils. And they rested on the Sabbath according to the commandment.

John

19:38 After this, Joseph of Arimathea, being a disciple of Jesus, but secretly, for fear of the Jews, asked Pilate that he might take away the body of Jesus; and Pilate gave him permission. So he came and took the body of Jesus. **39** And Nicodemus, who at first came to Jesus by night, also came, bringing a mixture of myrrh and aloes, about a hundred pounds. **40** Then they took the body of Jesus, and bound it in strips of linen with the spices, as the custom of the Jews is to bury. **41** Now in the place where He was crucified there was a garden, and in the garden a new tomb in which no one had yet been laid. **42** So there they laid Jesus, because of the Jews' Preparation Day, for the tomb was nearby.

11.0   HE IS RISEN

John

Read the next four sentences **very carefully!** *Jesus* is telling us that *He* has raised *Himself* from the dead using a command given to *Him* by *His* Father.

John 10:17

"*Therefore My* Father loves *Me*, because—

I — lay down *My* life

—that—

I — may take *it again*.

18 *No one*—takes it *from Me*

—but—

I — lay it down *of Myself*.

I — have the power

—to— lay it down,

—and—

_I_ — _have the_ power

— _to take_ it again.

This command—

_I_ — _have_ received _from My_ Father."

11.1 Jesus is the True Shepherd
Matthew, Mark, Luke, John

Matthew

28:1 Now after the Sabbath, as the first day of the week began to dawn, Mary Magdalene and the other Mary came to see the tomb. **2** And behold, there was a great earthquake; for an angel of the Lord descended from heaven, and came and rolled back the stone from the door, and sat on it. **3** His countenance was like lightning, and his clothing as white as snow. **4** And the guards shook for fear of him, and became like dead men. **5** But *the angel answered and said to the women, "Do not be afraid, for I know that you seek Jesus who was crucified.* **6** *He is not here; for He is risen, as He said. Come, see the place where the Lord lay.* **7** *And go quickly and tell His disciples that He is risen from the dead, and indeed He is going before you into Galilee; there you will see Him. Behold, I have told you."* **8** So they went out quickly from the tomb with fear and great joy, and ran to bring His disciples word.

Mark

16:1 Now when the Sabbath was past, Mary Magdalene, Mary the mother of James, and Salome bought spices, that they might come and anoint Him. **2** Very early in the morning, on the first day of the week, they came to the tomb when the sun had risen.

3 And **they said among themselves, "Who will roll away the stone from the door of the tomb for us?"** **4** But when they looked up, they saw that the stone had been rolled away--for it was very large. **5** And entering the tomb, they saw a young man clothed in a long white robe sitting on the right side; and they were alarmed. 6 But _he said to them, "Do not be alarmed. You seek Jesus of Nazareth, who was crucified. He is risen! He is not here. See the place where they laid Him_. 7 But _go, tell His disciples--and Peter--that He is going before you into Galilee; there you will see Him, as He said to you_." 8 So they went out quickly and fled from the tomb, for they trembled and were amazed. And they said nothing to anyone, for they were afraid.

Luke

24:1 Now on the first day of the week, very early in the morning, they, and certain other women with them, came to the tomb bringing the spices which they had prepared.

2 But they found the stone rolled away from the tomb. **3** Then they went in and did not find the body of the Lord Jesus. **4** And it happened, as they were greatly perplexed about this, _that behold, two men stood by them in shining garments_. **5** Then, as they were afraid and bowed their faces to the earth, _they said to them, "Why do you seek the living among the dead? 6 He is not here, but is risen! Remember how He spoke to you when He was still in Galilee, 7 saying, 'The Son of Man must be delivered into the hands of sinful men, and be crucified, and the third day rise again.'_ " **8** And they remembered His words. **9** Then they returned from the tomb and told all these things to the eleven and to all the rest. **10** It was Mary Magdalene, Joanna, Mary the mother of James, and the other women with them, who told these things to the apostles. **11** And their words seemed to them like idle tales, and they did not believe them. **12** But Peter arose and ran to the tomb; and stooping down, he saw the linen cloths lying by themselves; and he departed, marveling to himself at what had happened.

John

20:1 Now on the first day of the week Mary Magdalene went to the tomb early, while it was still dark, and saw that the stone had been taken away from the tomb. **2** Then she ran and came to Simon Peter, and to the other disciple, whom Jesus loved, and said to them, "They have taken away the Lord out of the tomb, and we do not know where they have laid Him." **3** Peter therefore went out, and the other disciple, and were going to the tomb. **4** So they both ran together, and the other disciple outran Peter and came to the tomb first. **5** And he, stooping down and looking in, saw the linen cloths lying there; yet he did not go in. **6** Then Simon Peter came, following him, and went into the tomb; and he saw the linen cloths lying there, **7** and the handkerchief that had been around His head, not lying with the linen cloths, but folded together in a place by itself. **8** Then the other disciple, who came to the tomb first, went in also; and he saw and believed.

9 *For as yet they did not know the Scripture, that* He *must* rise again *from the* dead.

10 Then the disciples went away again to their own homes.

12.0   MARY MAGDALENE SEES THE RISEN LORD

Mark, John

Mark

16:9 Now when He rose early on the first day of the week, He appeared first to Mary Magdalene, out of whom He had cast seven demons. **10** She went and told those who had been with Him, as they mourned and wept. **11** And when they heard that He was alive and had been seen by her, they did not believe.

John

20:11 But Mary stood outside by the tomb weeping, and as she wept she stooped down and looked into the tomb. **12** And she saw two angels in white sitting, one at the head and the other at the feet, where the body of Jesus had lain. **13** Then *they said to her, "Woman, why are you weeping?"* She said to them, "**Because they have taken away my Lord, and I do not know where they have laid Him.**" **14** Now when she had said this, she turned around and saw Jesus standing there, and did not know that it was Jesus.

15 *Jesus said to her, "Woman, why are you weeping? Whom are you seeking?"* She, supposing Him to be the gardener, said to Him, "Sir, if You have carried *Him* away, tell me where You have laid *Him*, and I will take *Him* away." **16** *Jesus said to her, "Mary!"* She turned and said to *Him*, "*Rabboni*!" (which is to say, Teacher). **17** *Jesus said to her, "Do not cling to Me, for I have not yet ascended to My Father; but go to My brethren and say to them, 'I am ascending to My Father and your Father, and to My God and your God.'"* **18** Mary Magdalene came and told the disciples that she had seen the Lord, and that He had spoken these things to her.

13.0   JESUS APPEARS TO HIS DISCIPLES
Luke, John

Luke

24:36 Now as they said these things, <u>*Jesus Himself* stood in the midst of them, and said to them</u>, "<u>*Peace to you.*</u>" **37** But they were terrified and frightened, and supposed they had seen a spirit. **38** And <u>*He* said to them,</u> "<u>*Why are you troubled*</u>? And <u>why do doubts arise in your hearts</u>? **39** <u>*Behold My hands and My feet, that it is I Myself*. Handle Me and see, for a spirit does not have flesh and bones as you see I have</u>." **40** When <u>*He* had said this, *He* showed them *His hands* and *His feet*</u>. **41** But while they still did not believe for joy, and marveled, <u>*He* said to them</u>, "<u>*Have you any food here*</u>?" **42** So they gave Him a piece of a broiled fish and some honeycomb. **43** And <u>*He* took it and ate in their presence</u>.

John

20:19 Then, the same day at evening, being the first day of the week, when the doors were shut where the disciples were assembled, for fear of the Jews, <u>*Jesus* came and stood in the midst, and said to them</u>, "<u>*Peace be with you.*</u>" **20** When <u>*He* had said this, *He* showed them *His hands* and *His side*</u>. Then the disciples were glad when they saw the Lord.

14.0 THE GREAT COMMISSION
Matthew, Mark, Luke, John

Matthew

28:19 *Go therefore and make disciples of all the nations, baptizing them in the name of the Father and of the Son and of the Holy Spirit,* 20 *teaching them to observe all things that I have commanded you; and lo, I am with you always, even to the end of the age."*

Mark

16:14 Later *He appeared to the eleven as they sat at the table; and He rebuked their unbelief and hardness of heart, because they did not believe those who had seen Him after He had risen.* 15 And *He said to them, "Go into all the world and preach the gospel to every creature.*

16 *He who believes and is baptized will be saved; but he who does not believe will be condemned.* 17 And *these signs will follow those who believe: In My name they will cast out demons; they will speak with new tongues;* 18 *they will take up serpents; and if they drink anything deadly, it will by no means hurt them; they will lay hands on the sick, and they will recover."*

Luke

24: 44 Then *He said to them, "These are the words which I spoke to you while I was still with you, that all things must be fulfilled which were written in the Law of Moses and the Prophets and the Psalms concerning Me."* **45** And *He* opened their understanding, *that they might* comprehend the Scriptures. **46** Then *He said to them, "Thus it is written, and thus it was necessary for the Christ to suffer and to rise from the* dead *the third day,* **47** *and that* repentance *and* remission of sins *should be preached in His name to all nations, beginning at Jerusalem.* **48** And *you are witnesses of these things.* **49** Behold, I send the Promise of My Father *upon you; but tarry in the city of Jerusalem until you are endued with power from on high."*

John

20: 21 So *Jesus said to them again, "Peace to you! As the Father has sent Me, I also send you."* **22** And *when He had said this, He breathed on them, and said to them, "Receive the Holy Spirit.* **23** *If you forgive the sins of any, they are forgiven them; if you retain the sins of any, they are retained."*

John 20: 30 And truly Jesus did many other signs in the presence of His disciples, which are not written in this book; **31** but these are written that you may believe that Jesus is the Christ, the Son of God, and that believing you may have life in His name.

John 21: 25 And there are also many other things that Jesus did, which if they were written one by one, I suppose that even the world itself could not contain the books that would be written.

Amen.

15.0 FINAL AUTHORITY

I'm glad you came to this page, because I've got some very important things to talk with you about. You are here not because you planned to be here, but because you were predestined to be here. That's right, at this very page your life is changed because you no longer could say, " I didn't know ". You are not alone in knowing that there is someone greater than yourself and He orders each of our steps. You may have seen the books cover, or the first pages in which God said, Hear Him! But what called you here is not by accident, it's His will for your life. What you have passed by to get here is a story that if you did know, it was never complete. Why? Because, from the first page, to this page is a story that Jesus Christ gave me to transcribe for Him. I thought I knew everything about Him, until I asked God to show me something He had not shown anyone else. It was in a dream that He showed me, and my life has never been the same.

I was standing behind a crowd of people who had their backs to me and they were watching something I couldn't see. They were all very noisy then all of a sudden they were quiet and moved apart as if someone wanted to get through. The crowd opened up and there standing was what God had never showed anyone else.

You see, what He showed me was His Son on the way to be crucified.

I saw how beaten and unrecognizable He appeared, His face didn't look human. No description I've read in the Bible could have ever brought to me the sadness and anger I felt for Him. Even just writing about this caused me anguish beyond anything I've ever experienced. He truly did pay the price for our sins and I am writing this so you will know that His sorrow was not for Himself, but for us.

Then Jesus cried out and said, "He who believes in Me, believes not in Me but in Him who sent Me. And he who sees Me sees Him who sent Me. I have come as a light into the world, that whoever believes in Me should not abide in darkness. And if anyone hears My words and does not believe, I do not judge him; for I did not come to judge the world but to save the world. He who rejects Me, and does not receive My words, has that which judges him--the word that I have spoken will judge him in the last day. For I have not spoken on My own authority; but the Father who sent Me gave Me a command, what I should say and what I should speak. And I know that His command is everlasting life. Therefore, whatever I speak, just as the Father has told Me, so I speak." John 12: 44-50

A Proof of the Death of Christ

Dr. Stroud (On the Physiological Cause of the Death of Christ, London, 1847) basing his remarks on numerous postmortems, pronounced the opinion that here we had a proof of the death of Christ being due not to the effects of crucifixion but to "laceration or rupture of the heart" as a consequence of supreme mental agony and sorrow. It is well attested that usually the suffering on the cross was very prolonged. It often lasted two or three days, when death would supervene from exhaustion. There were no physical reasons why Christ should not have lived very much longer on the cross than He did. On the other hand, death caused by laceration of the heart in consequence of great mental suffering would be almost instantaneous. In such a case the phrase "of a broken heart," becomes literally true. The life blood flowing through the aperture or laceration into the pericardium or caul of the heart, being extravasated, soon coagulates into the red clot (blood) and the limpid serum (water). This accumulation in the heart-sac was released by the spear-thrust of the soldier (which here takes providentially the place of a postmortem without which it would have been impossible to determine the real cause of death), and from the gaping wound there flow the two component parts of blood distinctly visible.

Several distinguished physicians have accepted Dr. Stroud's argument, and some have strengthened it by the observation of additional symptoms. We may mention Dr. James Begbie, fellow and late president of the Royal College of Physicians of Edinburgh, Sir J. Y. Simpson, professor at the University of Edinburgh, and others (see Dr. Hanna, Our Lord's Life on Earth, Appendix I). The latter refers to the loud cry, mentioned by the Synoptists

Matthew 27:50 And Jesus cried out again with a loud voice, and yielded up His spirit.
Mark 15:37 And Jesus cried out with a loud voice, and breathed His last.

Luke 23:46 And when Jesus had cried out with a loud voice, He said, "Father, 'into Your hands I commit My spirit.' " Having said this, He breathed His last.

which preceded the actual death of Jesus, as a symptom characteristic of cases of "broken heart." He adds that Dr. Walshe, professor of medicine in University College, London, one of the greatest authorities on the diseases of the heart, says that a "piercing shriek" is always uttered in such cases immediately before the end.

While we may never reach a state of absolute certainty on this subject, there is no valid reason to deny the probability of this view of the death of Christ. It certainly gives a more solemn insight into Christ's spiritual anguish, "the travail of his soul" on our behalf, which weighed upon Him so heavily that long before the usual term of bodily and therefore endurable suffering of crucified persons Christ's loving heart broke, achieving the great atoning sacrifice for all mankind.

H. L. E. Luering

15.1 FINAL AUTHORITY RESTS

Now we come to the final section of this book, who is the final authority? This may come as a surprise to most of you who have born the burden of Jesus' trial through His suffering and death, to His resurrection. The reason God allowed you to be called to this level of understanding was for a very special reason. It is you who hold this book, you are the final person in the position of authority. For now you know Jesus as no one else could, how He has given Himself for your life. Yes, you have seen the facts and read the accounts of what He said and did for you and ALL mankind.

Now it is up to you to judge for yourself, is He ***innocent***? Is His sacrifice of His Life for Your sins worthy of His ***acceptance***, now and forever?

These are yes or no questions! It can only move you to a point in this life in which His ***acceptance*** as the Son of God will lead you onto the path of eternal life. Remember, He died for You, this is your greatest opportunity to show Him that His death will win the battle for your eternal life. He is asking You to join Him in this life and the life that never ends.

John 3: 16 *For* God *so loved the world that* He *gave* His *only begotten* Son, *that whoever* believes *in* Him *should not* perish *but have* everlasting life.

These things I have spoken to you in figurative language; but the time is coming when I will no longer speak to you in figurative language, but I will tell you plainly about the Father. In that day you will ask in My name, and I do not say to you that I shall pray the Father for you; for the Father Himself loves you, because you have loved Me, and have believed that I came forth from God. I came forth from the Father and have come into the world. Again, I leave the world and go to the Father.

His disciples said to Him, "See, now You are speaking plainly, and using no figure of speech! <u>Now we are sure that You know all things, and have no need that anyone should question You. By this we believe</u> that You came forth from God."

John 16: 25-31

Jesus answered them, "<u>*Do you now believe*</u>?"

As the FINAL AUTHORITY, "<u>*Do you now believe*</u>?"

The Best

Is Yet

To

Come

THIS PAGE DEDICATED TO

GERALDINE

www.ingramcontent.com/pod-product-compliance
Lightning Source LLC
Chambersburg PA
CBHW051721170526
45167CB00002B/750